Donna K. Maltese

When JESUS Speaks to an ANXIOUS HEART

DEVOTIONAL
JOURNAL

BARBOUR BOOKS
An Imprint of Barbour Publishing, Inc.

© 2018 by Barbour Publishing, Inc.

ISBN 978-1-64352-672-0

Published by Barbour Books, an imprint of Barbour Publishing, Inc., 1810 Barbour Drive, Uhrichsville, Ohio 44683, www.barbourbooks.com

Our mission is to inspire the world with the life-changing message of the Bible.

Member of the
Evangelical Christian
Publishers Association

Printed in China.

Introduction

Experts tell us that 85 percent of what we worry about never comes to pass. Yet knowing that statistic often doesn't seem to matter. We are too soon and too often filled with and reacting from anxieties—worries, concerns, fears, troubles, tension—before we even know they are upon us!

But God would have His people live a life free of such a state of mind, body, heart, soul, and spirit. To help you in that endeavor is *When Jesus Speaks to an Anxious Heart.* These readings are pathways to a calmer and thus more power-filled state of being, with Christ's love and concern for you at the core. Each reading is a reminder that there are things so much more powerful than your anxieties, things such as God's Word, the Holy Spirit, Christ's gift of salvation and grace, and your faith.

Jesus knows exactly what you're going through. He knows your past, present, and future, your hopes, dreams, and, yes, your worries. He also knows the best path for you—and your thoughts. So dig into His promises, His Word, and His passion to help you live the best life for His glory. Begin here, within these pages. And as you continue your journey to be the best you can be for Christ, may. . .

"The LORD bless you and keep you; the LORD make His face shine upon you, and be gracious to you; the LORD lift up His countenance upon you, and give you peace."
NUMBERS 6:24–26 NKJV

Relax in Me

"The eternal God is your refuge, and his everlasting arms are under you."
DEUTERONOMY 33:27 NLT

I am your eternal shelter. When you are in Me, nothing can ever harm you. So come. Come now in this very moment.

Make Me your refuge, your hiding place. Feel My left hand under your head, My right hand holding you close. Here, in Me, do not just rest—*relax*!

In My presence you have room to breathe. To just be. Let the world fall away. Know that I am holding you up, that I am with you no matter where you are, that I am all you need—all you will ever need—in this world and the next. For I am the one who continues to breathe life and love, and hope and joy, and rest into you, moment by moment.

Fill yourself with My Spirit and Light, and all apprehensions will fall away. For when I am filling you completely, there is no room for anything else.

Take Me at My Word. Come to Me now. Fall into My everlasting arms. Know for certain that I've got you. I'm holding on to you—mind, body, heart, spirit, and soul—and never letting go. All you need to do is rest, relax. And be. In Me.

[I can feel] his left hand under my head and his right hand embraces me!
SONG OF SOLOMON 2:6 AMPC

As Promised

The LORD kept his word and did for Sarah exactly what he had promised. She became pregnant, and she gave birth to a son for Abraham in his old age. This happened at just the time God had said it would. . . . And Sarah declared, "God has brought me laughter. All who hear about this will laugh with me."
GENESIS 21:1–2, 6 NLT

I am not like man, that I change My mind or break My promises. I am your friend, brother, the one who would lay down His life for you. So be assured, I will keep My word.

All the promises you read in My Word are yours to claim, to own, to build your life, trust, and hope on. I will do exactly what I have promised—no half measures, nothing left undone. I will in no way leave you hanging. Just trust that what I have said I will bring to pass.

My keeping these promises to you may appear impossible. But how or when they are to be fulfilled is no concern of yours. So do not allow all the what-ifs to cloud your thinking, your dreams, or your heart's desire. Just persevere. Rest in the assurance of My Word, and in My timing, things will happen—just as I said they would. Then you will be bubbling over with laughter—and those around you will laugh with you, saying, "Look what God has done in your life!"

Tap In and Rise Up

I also pray that you will understand the incredible greatness of God's power for us who believe him. This is the same mighty power that raised Christ from the dead and seated him in the place of honor at God's right hand in the heavenly realms.
EPHESIANS 1:19–20 NLT

Ah, My child. Do not despair. I know that at times you feel powerless. That you feel as if you are caught up in a society, a culture that does not understand you. Does not see you for who you truly are. This world in which you exist is not of your own making, although some situations you find yourself in may be. Either case, do not worry. Do not fret. For you have a source of power available to you. Otherworldly power. Power that can protect, save, and lift out of the fray.

You are a believer. And as such, you can tap into the amazing fount of God's power, the same power that brought Me, raised Me, lifted Me from the dead. This is the power that seated Me on the throne, to a place of honor, right next to God OUR Father!

So take heart. Tap in. Rise up. Know that there is a place for you with Me and our Father. A place reserved just for you!

Well Full of Hope

When the water was gone, she put the boy in the shade of a bush. Then she went and sat down by herself about a hundred yards away. "I don't want to watch the boy die," she said, as she burst into tears. But God heard the boy crying, and the angel of God called to Hagar from heaven, "Hagar, what's wrong? Do not be afraid!" . . . Then God opened Hagar's eyes, and she saw a well full of water.
GENESIS 21:15–17, 19 NLT

There may be days when all you want to do is sit down and cry. When all you can see is the situation before you, leaving you bereft of all hope.

I Myself have cried. I wept upon hearing of the death of My friend Lazarus. Upon seeing My friends overwhelmed by their own grief. Yet I have never lost hope.

So sit down and have a good cry if that's what you need. But do not linger in the wilderness into which you have aimlessly wandered. Take note of My presence. Call out My name. Upon hearing your cry, I will send My angels to you. And I will open your eyes. I will show you where to go to be refreshed, replenished. I will show you the abundance available to you, the well full of living water!

I will give you a future and a hope. For I have great plans for you!

Burden Bearer

"I took the world off your shoulders, freed you from a life of hard labor. You called to me in your pain; I got you out of a bad place. I answered you from where the thunder hides, I proved you at Meribah Fountain."

PSALM 81:6–7 MSG

I, Jesus, came down to earth and lived among you. I took all your burdens upon Myself. I freed you who were captive to the missteps that plagued you, kept from doing all that God had planned for you since the beginning of time.

You cried out for Me, and so I rescued you, brought you to a better place. I spoke to you from the mountains, showed you how to live, where to go when you needed to get closer to Me. I left the Holy Spirit with you, a personal guide to the most wonderful life you can live in the light.

But you refuse to remember. You continue to live as if all these things have not been done for you. You act as if the burdens in your life are ones you can actually bear. They are not! Come! Now! Bring all your cares and woes, your doubts and frustrations, your anxieties and fears to Me! Lay them down at My feet. Only *I* can pick up and bear such a load!

Then rise up anew. Breathe, live, love, and be whom you were created to be. A follower in and of Me, the Christ!

Expect a Miracle

And there was a woman who had had a flow of blood for twelve years. . . .
She had heard the reports concerning Jesus, and she came up behind Him in the throng
and touched His garment, for she kept saying, If I only touch His garments, I shall be
restored to health. And immediately her flow of blood was dried up at the source.
MARK 5:25, 27–29 AMPC

When you are feeling weak, know that I have the answer. That I can give you strength. That I can make you whole.

Be as the woman with the hemorrhage who allowed nothing to stand between us. Even though she was considered an outcast, that did not stop her from pressing in, pressing on, pressing Me. Even though she was physically weak, having bled for twelve years, she was spiritually strong. She had the faith that allows Me to work miracles, and the determination and perseverance to see miracles become reality.

She kept telling herself that I was her answer. I was her restorer. And that was what brought My power out of Myself and into her, healing her *instantly.*

Be such a woman of fearless faith. Be the one who perseveres. Reach out for My power. Be assured that I am the answer to your prayers. Get ready—and then expect a miracle.

The Amazing Paradox

We felt like we'd been sent to death row, that it was all over for us. As it turned out, it was the best thing that could have happened. Instead of trusting in our own strength or wits to get out of it, we were forced to trust God totally—not a bad idea since he's the God who raises the dead! And he did it, rescued us from certain doom. And he'll do it again, rescuing us as many times as we need rescuing.

2 CORINTHIANS 1:9–10 MSG

───◦·◆·◦───

The days when you may feel as if you're not going to make it, when you feel as if you are in the dark, those are the days that I can really shine!

That's the amazing paradox of a life lived in Me! The days that you think are the worst for you are actually the best for you. For that's when you are forced to trust in Me—totally! When you can't figure a way out, when you have no more strength or sanity left, when your emotions are on the edge, I can step in and rescue you! And I can do it over and over again.

So do not despair. Know that I have the power to rescue you, no matter how deep you get. Just keep that at the forefront of your mind and heart, and the next thing you know, instead of whistling in the dark you'll be praising in the light!

Crossroads

I [the Lord] will instruct you and teach you in the way you should go; I will counsel you with My eye upon you. Be not like the horse or the mule, which lack understanding, which must have their mouths held firm with bit and bridle, or else they will not come with you.
PSALM 32:8–9 AMPC

Each day you may find yourself at a crossroads, wondering which path to take. Sometimes your choice may seem like a small, almost insignificant decision. But in your walk with Me, every step you take counts. Every choice has its consequence.

Yet do not be anxious. Do not fret. Simply spend time in My Word and in My company. I, your teacher, will instruct you. Then you will learn who I am and know what I would have you do in each and every situation. But if at any time you are uncertain, pause at the crossroads. Ask Me which way you should go. Then, only when you clearly hear My voice, choose your path and step out in faith. Do not be slow. Do not have the stubbornness of a mule. But take courage, be bold, filled with the assurance that I have already gone ahead and paved the way.

If you do not hear My voice, wait upon Me. Know there is a reason your feet are stayed. I have My eye upon you. And I will not lead you into evil, only good. Rest in that knowledge.

Blessed Peacemaker

*Blessed (enjoying enviable happiness, spiritually prosperous—with life-joy and satisfaction
in God's favor and salvation, regardless of their outward conditions) are the makers
and maintainers of peace, for they shall be called the sons of God!*
MATTHEW 5:9 AMPC

If you are unsettled in mind, heart, spirit, and soul, stop. Take some moments to search within. See if there is any unwillingness to forgive lingering there. If there are any grudges against people who have put you out in some way. Any grievance that you are still harboring in your heart.

Then come to Me. I am the Prince of Peace. I can heal any breach—no matter how deep, no matter how old. But to heal you, you must come.

Perhaps this unsettled feeling has nothing to do with another person. Perhaps it is something that you have yet to forgive yourself for. Perhaps it is something that you have yet to admit to yourself. Or don't want to tell Me about.

Child, know that I already know everything you are made of. I already know everything you have already done. And I love you more than you can imagine. So do not despair. There is nothing you can do that can remove My love from you.

So look. Come. Rest in My presence. Revel in and absorb My abundant peace. Then go out into your world, knowing that I, the healer of breaches, walk with you; and go, do likewise, following in My steps, maintaining the peace.

Choose Love

Jesus said, " 'Love the Lord your God with all your passion and prayer
and intelligence.' This is the most important, the first on any list. But there is
a second to set alongside it: 'Love others as well as you love yourself.' "
MATTHEW 22:37–39 MSG

Love. Love. Love. That is My word and command for you today—and every day. First, love Me. With all that you are—heart, mind, body, soul, strength, spirit. Next, love yourself. For how can you love and show compassion to others if you do not love and show compassion to yourself?

This is your choice—to love or not to love—every moment of every day. I have even given you an example to follow.

I loved you from the very beginning, before you were even formed, before you loved Me. I continued to love you when you denied Me, wronged Me, hurt Me. And I will continue to love you—no matter where you go or what you do.

Trust that I pour out upon you an abundance of love, enough love to overflow you and for you to extend to yourself and others. And all you need to do to receive it is to recognize, and to seek Me. I am here. I am waiting. I am love.

"If you love me, show it by doing what I've told you."
JOHN 14:15 MSG

Praise the Lord

*Let all that I am praise the LORD; may I never forget the good things he does
for me. He forgives all my sins and heals all my diseases. . . . He has removed
our sins as far from us as the east is from the west.*
PSALM 103:2–3, 12 NLT

Are you still holding on to how you missed the mark (sinned) a day, week, month, year, decade ago? My child, do not do this to yourself! Do not continually muse over your misdeeds, mutter over how you continue to make the same mistake, or, even worse, alienate yourself from Me because you don't feel worthy to be in My presence.

Stop in this moment. Know that I have already forgiven you. For My eye is constantly upon you, examining your heart, looking to see how you are, concerned for your being, like a mother who looks out for her precious child. I know you will make mistakes. And My plan has already allowed for them. Thus, understand and know that I no longer see your sins. In fact, I have removed them from you. So think of them no more, for to do so diffuses My strength and power within you. And I have many things for you to do in My name.

May all that you are praise Me as you realize what I have done for you!

Be Confident

Delight yourself also in the Lord, and He will give you the desires and secret petitions of your heart. Commit your way to the Lord [roll and repose each care of your load on Him]; trust (lean on, rely on, and be confident) also in Him and He will bring it to pass.
PSALM 37:4–5 AMPC

———◦◆◦———

I do not want to be a part of your daily drudge, like a meeting you have to attend. I want you to run to Me, to want to be with Me, like a child longing to be in her mother's presence, bursting with joy as she scrambles up onto her lap, leans back against her breast, and finds a peace and joy like no other.

Come to Me like that little child. Delight in My company. Tell Me your plans, your dreams. Leave with Me all your worries and what-ifs. I will take care of them in good order. Then trust Me to bring your desires to pass in the way that best serves you, Me, and God's grand plan. For as you love Me more and more, slowly My desires are what you grow to desire.

Remember to rely on Me more than yourself and those around you. Trust in Me more than you do the temporal things and beings in your world. Remember that I have so many more allies at My disposal, angels who run to do My bidding. Be confident in all this.

Prayers and Praise

"You will not have to fight this battle. Take up your positions; stand firm and see the deliverance the LORD will give you. . . . Do not be afraid; do not be discouraged. Go out to face them tomorrow, and the LORD will be with you."

2 CHRONICLES 20:17 NIV

The greatest powers you have at your disposal are prayer and praise. Pray when the world seems to be crashing down on you, when you feel as if you have nowhere to turn, when everything seems to be against you—and you will come into the awareness that I am with you. Lift your voice in praise that with Me by your side, nothing can destroy you.

For you need not fight any battles when I am with you. All you have to do is stand there. Keep your feet planted. Be calm. And in that state My amazing power can and will work with you and deliver you.

So as I have said many times, do not be afraid. Do not lose courage or hope. Go out and face the situation, resting and relaxing in the peace and strength that comes from knowing that I am—and will be—with you. You couldn't lose Me if you tried! I will bring you victory as you turn your prayers into praise over the rewards you will soon be reaping!

Desired Haven

Then they cry to the Lord in their trouble, and He brings them out of their distresses.
He hushes the storm to a calm and to a gentle whisper, so that the waves of the sea are still.
Then the men are glad because of the calm, and He brings them to their desired haven.
PSALM 107:28–30 AMPC

How can I help you unless you cry out to Me to be saved?

So many times you forget about Me. You try to do things in your own power, under your own steam. And before you know it, you have drifted away and are soon drowning in dilemmas, desperate to find a way out, no matter how foolish or harmful to yourself and perhaps others. As you tread water, gulping down mouthfuls of angst-filled thoughts, you remember and come to Me. You cry and I immediately respond and calm the storm. Soon the wind has lessened and the waves are as still as a pond. You feel the joy you've been longing for. And I have the desire of My own heart well secured within My arms.

Filled once again with calm, you feel the joy of My love and protection. And before you know it, I have brought you exactly where you desired to be from the beginning. With Me.

All Ways, All Days

But I will sing of Your mighty strength and power; yes, I will sing aloud of Your mercy and loving-kindness in the morning; for You have been to me a defense (a fortress and a high tower) and a refuge in the day of my distress.
PSALM 59:16 AMPC

Yes, sing, sing, sing of My strength and power. Shout about My mercy, forgiveness, and overflowing love for you. And watch walls as thick as Jericho tumble down, because your faith united with My power can destroy any barriers you come up against.

Know that I am what stands between you and the things that would harm you. When you come to Me, when you realize My presence, you are assured of My protection. It is only when you lose that awareness of Me that you begin to fear and fret.

But as soon as you begin to turn toward Me, to trust Me, to reach out your hand and put it in My own, you find a strength that is not your own, a confidence that is otherworldly, an infusion of love that is overwhelming, and a peace of mind, heart, body, soul, and spirit that is unimaginable.

So sing. Praise. Reach out your hand. Feel My power entering you. And know that I stand with you in all ways, all days.

From Discord to Delight

"I take joy in doing your will, my God,
for your instructions are written on my heart."
PSALM 40:8 NLT

Feeling unsettled? Pause in your daily doings and get away by yourself, even if only for a few moments. Prayerfully look within. See where you may be walking out of step with the Holy Spirit I have left for you. He is your gift, to help you find your way.

When you are not following the Spirit's promptings, when you are not heeding His whispers of *"Pssst. This way! Come this way!"* you will feel the otherworldly discord in every area of your life, leading to confusion, and the confusion to anxiety.

Have the promptings you received not made sense to you with your limited thinking? Were you not exactly sure whose voice you were hearing? Whatever the case, have no fear. Call Me and I will come near. I will sidle up beside you, help you find your footing again. I will help you home in on the true voice so that you can get out of your current wilderness and find your way back to your Promised Land. I am your compass and your guide, always pointing you in the right direction so that there is harmony in your life. So that you will no longer feel the discord but only the joy in doing the will of your Lord.

Come away with Me. Let's consider. Let's move from discord to delight.

Relief from Unbelief

When doubts filled my mind, your comfort gave me renewed hope and cheer. . . .
The LORD is my fortress; my God is the mighty rock where I hide.
PSALM 94:19, 22 NLT

Why oh why are you so riddled with doubts about Me, My power, My strength, My love, My ability, My longing to help you, and even at times My very existence? Even worse, why do you hide those doubts from Me?

Have you not heard the story of the man whose boy needed healing? The one who asked Me to take pity on him and his son and pleaded, "If there's anything you can do, please help us"?

My reply was and still is to all doubters: Anything and everything is possible for the one who believes—in Me, My power, My strength, My longing to help you, My love, My ability.

So come to Me now, My beloved, with all your doubts and fears. Spill them out. Spell them out. Then ask Me to help you increase your belief in Me, to teach you how to overcome any stumbling blocks in your faith. For in doing so, you will immediately find relief from your suffering. You will sense My Spirit. You will have a new sense of hope and cheer as I take you by the hand and lift you to your feet.

Long Way Around

God did not lead them by way of the land of the Philistines, although that was near; for God said, "Lest perhaps the people change their minds when they see war, and return to Egypt." So God led the people around by way of the wilderness of the Red Sea.

EXODUS 13:17–18 NKJV

———◦•◦———

You are anxious, ready to begin something new, take on a fresh challenge. Yet things are not falling into place. Perhaps it is because you are not yet ready for the path chosen.

So do not wring your hands, let frustration take hold, or become impatient. Instead, know that I see you and your situation. I know you inside out, from beginning to end. I know what you think, say, and do. I know your desires and the plan that has been in place for you since time began. So calm your restlessness. Soothe yourself with the knowledge that all is falling into place for you. It may appear to be the long way, but it's the right way. What you desire will come to pass—in My time, not yours.

Your job is to grow stronger, increase in knowledge, determination, and confidence, and continually look to Me for the next step. Your desires and dreams *will* become reality. In fact, I have already gone ahead to prepare the way. Everything is under control. So, for now, commit all your plans to Me. Then just rest and wait.

Distracted with God

Practically everything that goes on in the world—wanting your own way,
wanting everything for yourself, wanting to appear important—has nothing to do
with the Father. It just isolates you from him. The world and all its wanting, wanting,
wanting is on the way out—but whoever does what God wants is set for eternity.

1 JOHN 2:16–17 MSG

So many things surrounding you are vying for your attention. But I would have you keep your eyes on Me.

The world will entice you with things it says you should have. Just as the apple enticed your ancient forbearers. So do not be distracted by or give in to those physical cravings. Nor long for all those shiny things the world has to offer. Nor demand your own way in every situation. All those things draw you further and further away from Me and deeper and deeper down the roads that will lead you astray—and worse.

Instead, look to Me. Desire Me. Distract yourself with Me. Demand My way in every situation. That will lead you to eternal joy. That will bring you close to Me, My Word, and My will and provide you with incomparable riches beyond imagining. Do not love the world and everything that is in it. Love Me and all that I am.

Well on the Wave

Peter went over the side of the boat and walked on the water toward Jesus.
But when he saw the strong wind and the waves, he was terrified and began to sink.
MATTHEW 14:29–30 NLT

You are well on your way. You have taken a great leap of faith. You have determined to take a risk, to get out of a current situation and try something that takes a great deal of belief in Me. But somewhere along the line, the supposed reality of what you are doing comes to the forefront of your mind. Soon, the what-if questions—your own or those of others—begin to take over all your thoughts, setting off alarms throughout your entire being. The next thing you know, you have taken your eyes off Me—Lord of impossibilities—and begin to falter.

So it has been with other followers. Peter himself, when walking toward Me upon the sea, turned his attention from Me and onto the tumultuous wind and waves. Terror set in, his faith began to waver, and he began to sink.

Keep your eyes on Me. Know I am on the rough seas with you. I will never let you sink. When you feel yourself wavering, all you need to do is call out to Me, and I will grab you immediately and calm the wind and waters within and without. For I AM the Son of God!

Divine Interruptions

*The LORD gave this message to Jonah son of Amittai: "Get up and go to the great city of Nineveh. . . ."
But Jonah got up and went in the opposite direction to get away from the LORD. . . . But the LORD
hurled a powerful wind over the sea, causing a violent storm that threatened to break the ship apart.*
JONAH 1:1–4 NLT

You may feel as if your days are filled with interruptions, things, or events that are keeping you from living your "real" life. Take heart. Relax. Because those interruptions *are* your real life.

Jonah must have felt frustrated when My Father told him to ignore his "real" life and go to Nineveh. So he went the other way, determined to do what he wanted to do—and ended up suffering, as did his fellow shipmates, for ignoring the divine interruption. In the end, he wound up in Nineveh anyway, just as God had planned.

And that's the point. Your life is God's plan—not your own. There are lessons you are meant to learn. So do not allow frustration to take hold when you find your life interrupted. Do not disobey when God speaks a new plan into your life. Instead, be vigilant in seeking His face, obeying His directive, and keeping yourself and life in line with God's plan. In doing so, God knows how many storms you will avoid.

In My Hand

[Shadrach, Meshach, and Abed-Nego] were cast into the midst of the burning fiery furnace. . . . [Then Nebuchadnezzar said], "I see four men loose, walking in the midst of the fire; and they are not hurt, and the form of the fourth is like the Son of God." . . . Then Shadrach, Meshach, and Abed-Nego came from the midst of the fire. . . . The fire had no power; the hair of their head was not singed nor were their garments affected, and the smell of fire was not on them.

DANIEL 3:21, 25–27 NKJV

In this world there are many ways to suffer. I Myself writhed beneath the whip and upon the cross in pain and agony. I was rejected by family, friends, disciples, people. I was despised, beaten, judged. Yet I remained faithful to and in our Father.

I know what you are going through. I know and have felt every wound you have ever received, from birth to this very moment. Because of your faith in Me, I have walked through the fire with you. And because I was with you, the fire—your circumstance—has no real power.

So fear nothing. Do not worry—no matter how dire the situation may seem. For nothing can ever touch you when you are in My hand.

Power of Promises

*Through these [God's own glory and goodness] he has given us his very great and precious
promises, so that through them you may participate in the divine nature,
having escaped the corruption in the world caused by evil desires.*

2 PETER 1:4 NIV

What precious promises you have at your disposal! Claim them! Take them! Make them your very own! Allow them to permeate your very being!

I have promised to forgive your sins. That's why I took on the form of a man, came to earth, healed, helped, bled, died, and was raised up. I was the example for you to follow. So claim first the blessing of pardoned missteps!

When I departed, I sent you the Holy Spirit to live within you, to be your Comforter, Counselor, Helper, and Strengthener. He is the one who can teach you all you need to know to live the life you were created to live. Claim the Counselor who will lead you to places you never dreamed or imagined.

Take hold of the divine nature that is yours when you claim each of God's promises. And you will be freed from all the things that threatened to snare you, hold you down, trip you up, weigh you down, and keep you from flying like God's eagle.

Your Strength and Shield

Blessed be the Lord, because He has heard the voice of my supplications. The Lord is my Strength and my [impenetrable] Shield; my heart trusts in, relies on, and confidently leans on Him, and I am helped; therefore my heart greatly rejoices, and with my song will I praise Him.
PSALM 28:6–7 AMPC

I am your shield, the defense that surrounds you, protecting you from things seen and unseen. I have heard your cries and have come to secure you, to ensure you are not supplanted by those things that would bring you harm. See Me fortifying you, safeguarding you. I am an impenetrable wall of love, mercy, and strength. Abiding in Me, you can take your stand. Nothing can harm you here.

There is no need for you to fight—I, your firm foundation, your rock, your buttress, your prince, am fighting for you. You need only stand still and see Me deliver you.

So there's no need to run, fret, cry, or freeze. Just relax, trust, and sense My never-ending presence, My mobile hedge of protection that can never be destroyed. Do not doubt Me in this. For within this wall of security lies your freedom and strength, your confidence and well-being.

Save Your people and bless Your heritage;
nourish and shepherd them and carry them forever.
PSALM 28:9 AMPC

At Your Word

He said to Simon, "Launch out into the deep and let down your nets for a catch."
But Simon answered and said to Him, "Master, we have toiled all night and caught
nothing; nevertheless at Your word I will let down the net." And when they had
done this, they caught a great number of fish, and their net was breaking.
LUKE 5:4–6 NKJV

I am your guide, your path, the one who leads you to what you are looking for. Are you following Me? Are you listening to My Word, My whispers, My voice? And after you hear, do you heed what I say? Do you step out in faith and do what I tell you even though, in the world's eyes, My direction seems foolish at best?

Put yourself before Me. Lie back in the sunlight of My presence. Breathe in the warmth of My love. Allow your self-will to lessen and My will to increase.

For I am all you ever need. I am your source and supply.

Without Me, you stress and strain, you overwork, you reap little. But with Me, heeding My direction, you find what you need and more!

Learn from My disciples. Take My Word to heart. Go deep. And you will have more than you could ever think, dream, hope, or imagine. Trust Me in this.

Finding Life

*Whoever goes hunting for what is
right and kind finds life itself—glorious life!*
PROVERBS 21:21 MSG

I am interested in your life. Every tear, every smile, every joy, every heartache. I am looking to connect with you in everything you experience—every sunset you see, rainbow you chase, and storm cloud you fear. As you seek Me, I seek you. To chat. To walk. To dream.

So seek Me as ardently as I seek you. For I am always near, just waiting for you to respond to My knock, to open the door and eat with Me. It is then you will find and uncover the life you were born, made, meant to live. It is then you will find the way, the truth, and the life.

When you search for, find, and recover Me, when you bring Me into your life, you will be unable to contain your joy. You, like David, will break forth in dancing, singing, and praising Me with all your might. You will be celebrating in the kingdom of God.

---

*Behold, I stand at the door and knock; if anyone hears and listens to and heeds My voice
and opens the door, I will come in to him and will eat with him, and he [will eat] with Me.
He who overcomes (is victorious), I will grant him to sit beside Me on My throne, as I
Myself overcame (was victorious) and sat down beside My Father on His throne.*
REVELATION 3:20–21 AMPC

The Love and Life

"You're familiar with the old written law, 'Love your friend,' and its unwritten companion, 'Hate your enemy.' I'm challenging that. I'm telling you to love your enemies. Let them bring out the best in you, not the worst. When someone gives you a hard time, respond with the energies of prayer, for then you are working out of your true selves, your God-created selves. This is what God does. He gives his best—the sun to warm and the rain to nourish—to everyone, regardless: the good and bad, the nice and nasty."
MATTHEW 5:43–45 MSG

I would have you do the opposite of not only what the world would have you do but what the old eye-for-an-eye law would have you do. I want you to love not only your friends but your enemies.

What a way to change to world! What a way to make believers out of nonbelievers! Here is your chance to set society on its heels, to catch troublemakers off guard, to be the best I've created you to be.

This is not meant to take you out of your comfort zone but to bring you into the realization of who you really are. You are the follower of the One who loves the good and the bad, the problem and the solution, the challenge and the reward. The One who died for all. This is your chance to emulate Me—the Love and Life of the world.

Provision in Retreat

And after the earthquake a fire, but the Lord was not in the fire; and after the fire [a sound of gentle stillness and] a still, small voice. When Elijah heard the voice, he wrapped his face in his mantle and went out and stood in the entrance of the cave. And behold, there came a voice to him.
1 KINGS 19:12–13 AMPC

My servants, My brave ones, will not be left in want. Know this.

When you are weary, discouraged, forlorn, depressed. When you have retreated, when you have run for your life into the wilderness, I will provide for you, succor you, until you are ready to stand in My power again.

Was it not done for Elijah who, upon threat of his life, ran into the desert, asked Me to take his life, and then fell asleep? Did the angel of the Lord not give him food and water, the provision of which gave him new strength, allowing him to travel for forty days and nights to the mountain of God? Did he not then find Me in the still, small voice?

Learn from this. If you are weary, depressed, and despondent, sit and rest while I provide for you until you have regained strength, confidence, and hope and are ready to rise again, come to Me, and find your new direction—even if it's only to go back the way you came.

Bask in the Son-shine

"Look at the lilies and how they grow. They don't work or make their clothing, yet Solomon in all his glory was not dressed as beautifully as they are. And if God cares so wonderfully for flowers that are here today and thrown into the fire tomorrow, he will certainly care for you. Why do you have so little faith?"
LUKE 12:27–28 NLT

Stress and strain are for nonbelievers, not you. You are to be like the lily. Consider that flower. How it grows up into what it has already been designed to be. There is no struggle, no stress, no strain. It neither toils nor spins. Instead it just basks in the sunshine, drinks in the water, feeds off the soil, and takes in the air. So should it be with you.

Do not struggle. Simply allow yourself to grow up into what you have been created to be—a child of God. Consider how you do not need to work at this. Simply bask in the Son-shine. Drink in the living water. Feed off and be grounded in the soil of the Word. And take in the counsel of the Holy Spirit.

Trust Me in all this and you will find your life blessed, your growth unbounded, and your leaves green, bearing fruit regardless of the weather—inside and out.

I Am There

My help comes from the LORD, who made heaven and earth! He will not let you stumble; the one who watches over you will not slumber. Indeed, he who watches over Israel never slumbers or sleeps. The LORD himself watches over you! The LORD stands beside you as your protective shade.

PSALM 121:2–5 NLT

———◦•◦———

I never sleep. No matter when you seek Me, you will find Me, waiting, watching. No matter where you are, I am with you. When you call Me, it's not so much that I have not been with you, but that, because you have called, you have become more aware of My existence.

Remember, I have said that I will never leave you nor forsake you. Live in the truth of that promise, that knowledge. You can neither outlive, outrun, or outpace Me. For I am everywhere, in all things. It is in Me that you move, live, and have your very being.

So if you wake up in the middle of the night, speak to Me. I am there, longing to commune with you. If you are far away from home, never fear. I am where you are. If you have drifted away from My Spirit, afraid I will not recognize your voice, speak anyway, for I am listening. And I will answer. Nothing can separate Me or My love from you. Rest in this. Let it give you peace.

Forgetting and Forgiving

I do not consider, brethren, that I have captured and made it my own [yet];
but one thing I do [it is my one aspiration]: forgetting what lies
behind and straining forward to what lies ahead.
PHILIPPIANS 3:13 AMPC

Hush. Quiet. Let us sit. And remember. Pause. And forget. And forgive all those things that are best left behind. For they only hinder your progress forward and weigh you down in the present.

Old grudges. Painful experiences. Misunderstandings. Insults and injuries. Misplaced advice. Do not ruminate on them. Do not try to figure out how they happened or what you could have done to prevent them. Do not torture yourself with "If only I could have said this" or "If only I had done that." Just leave those experiences and the pain they caused at the point of their occurrence. And let the wounds remain there as well.

Imitate Me. Walk as I walked, unhindered. Forgetting and forgiving the betrayals, rejections, wounds, and lies of friends, family, and followers of whom more was expected. I even forgot and forgave the actions of those from whom no kindness or allegiance was expected.

Stop looking back, and look forward to what lies ahead. Let the past remain in the past, and embrace the freedom and joy that action gives you!

Worth Your While

Then the LORD said to Moses, "Look, I have specifically chosen Bezalel son of Uri, grandson of Hur, of the tribe of Judah. I have filled him with the Spirit of God, giving him great wisdom, ability, and expertise in all kinds of crafts. He is a master craftsman."
EXODUS 31:1–4 NLT

You have been given a special talent, an ability, a gift. Use it for My glory.

God has filled you with His Spirit, with His wisdom to do what no one else can do. And all in accordance with His plan and purpose. This talent comes with a passion. For it you need persistence. So look to Me. I will help you to keep on keeping on.

Do not allow others to dissuade you from plying your gift. Find a way to feed the passion for the craft that only your hands can undertake. Do not let your hands lie limp. But take up the task, keep at it, practice. And as you do so, you will improve. It will become worth your while. And sooner or later, it will reach the right hearts, find its own path, take on a life of its own.

Whatever you do, do not let circumstances dictate the work of your hands. Find a way to use what you've been given, to do what you've been appointed to do, in whatever way possible, be it little or small. And Father God will be glorified.

Be Still

The Lord of hosts is with us; the God of Jacob is our Refuge (our Fortress
and High Tower). Selah [pause, and calmly think of that]! . . . Let be
and be still, and know (recognize and understand) that I am God.
PSALM 46:7, 10 AMPC

―――⊙◆⊙―――

It is in the stillness that you hear, that you know, that you feel who I truly am.

So be still. Allow your hands to sit quietly in your lap. Relax your jaw, neck, shoulders, back—every part of your being, from the top of your hairs, which I have counted, to the tips of your toes, which I have formed, molded, and shaped.

Allow your breath to become slow and steady, a reminder of the undulating waves that softly break upon the shore and then drift back to the sea. Become aware of the rhythm, the cycle that all creation dances to.

Now that your body is still, turn your thoughts to Me. Sink into Me. Lean back against Me and feel My chest move up and down with each breath. Be filled with the light of My presence as we sit together, you and I, in the stillness of time, space, and spirit.

Yes, I am with you. You are secure in My arms. So rest easy. Know, recognize, understand that I am the very air you breathe and all that you need. Be still. And know.

Goodness in the Land of the Living

[What, what would have become of me] had I not believed that I would see the Lord's goodness in the land of the living! Wait and hope for and expect the Lord; be brave and of good courage and let your heart be stout and enduring. Yes, wait for and hope for and expect the Lord.
PSALM 27:13–14 AMPC

———◦◆◦———

I am doing something in your life, something that you cannot yet see. Know that all will be well. All is meant for good.

Do not despair. For in doing so, you distance yourself from Me. Instead, pray. There is supernatural power there. Have faith that all will be well. That you will see My goodness in your life.

Wait. Hope. Expect. Keep up your courage. Be patient. Have confidence. Trust that I am working, no matter how difficult things may seem. Remember that I see far beyond time and space. I know what lies ahead for you. And it is all for good. There is nothing to fear. No reason to fret. A new beginning lies before you. Beyond this point are things you never imagined or dreamed, things to give you hope, joy, and song. For now, hang on to My Word. Know the answers are there, awaiting your prayer. Abide in My light and presence. And I will strengthen you with My divine and eternal companionship.

Angels to Keep You

For He shall give His angels charge over you, to keep you in all your ways.
In their hands they shall bear you up, lest you dash your foot against a stone.
PSALM 91:11–12 NKJV

You are at a crossroads. A choice needs to be made. Not sure what foot to put forward, you hesitate. And soon find yourself rooted to the spot.

Come close. So close that you are in Me and I am in you. Here, there is no reason to waver nor to stand still. Simply ask Me for whatever wisdom you need. Heed My voice.

Petition Me for protection upon the way. Know that I am in charge of all nature. I command the wind and the waves. When you dwell in the secret place—My presence—you are well protected. Trusting in Me, nothing can harm you. You cannot make a misstep. Because I love you like no other, I have sent My angels to keep you, guard you, rescue you, lift you.

Refuse to let worries, frets, anxieties keep you from My power and peace. Instead, embrace your walk with Me with a new confidence. Step out in faith. Begin where you are. Know that because you trust and rely on Me, I will never let you go. I will not only rescue and protect you, guard and keep you, but adore and honor you.

Take your first step. And walk with Me.

Look Up!

But those who wait for the Lord [who expect, look for, and hope in Him] shall change and renew their strength and power; they shall lift their wings and mount up [close to God] as eagles [mount up to the sun]; they shall run and not be weary, they shall walk and not faint or become tired.
ISAIAH 40:31 AMPC

Your eyes are looking down. Look up! See Me! I am riding high in the heavens above you!

I have already delivered you, redeemed your life, and I will do so again and again, a thousand times. But you must look to Me. Wait for Me. Expect Me to move in your life!

When you do, you will find the power to lift your own wings, to mount up close to Me—God's Son—as an eagle would mount up to the sun. You will have untold energy so that you can run, walk, leap and not become tired or grow weak.

As God took care of His people in the wilderness, so I will take care of you. As He protected them, guarding them with His own eyes, so will I guard you. So mount up with Me. Ride the wind with Me. Rise above your problems, your worries, your heartaches, your mistakes. Fly above those who mock, misunderstand, and misjudge you.

Take a ride with Me into the heavens and see a whole new world, a new way of looking up!

Peace, Light, and Life. . .to Have and Hold

The Lord bless you and watch, guard, and keep you; the Lord make His face to shine upon and enlighten you and be gracious (kind, merciful, and giving favor) to you; the Lord lift up His [approving] countenance upon you and give you peace (tranquility of heart and life continually).
NUMBERS 6:24–26 AMPC

Peace is a treasure, a value beyond compare. Yet it is often pirated by conditions within and without. Do not look to the externals over which you have no control. No peace lies in putting your trust and confidence there. Let outside circumstances drift away, apart from your heart, spirit, soul, and mind.

Face what is happening within. Speak to your fears, worries, frets, and anxieties—in My name! And they will dissipate. Replace them with My Word. Believe in the promises that I will never leave nor forsake you; that I rule all things; that I am the source of all living beings and have powers beyond compare; that I am the beginning and the end.

Rest in the reality of My hand within your own, My whisper in your ear, My lips upon your cheek. You are Mine. Trust Me for all things. And My peace, light, and life will be yours to have and to hold.

Ask, Seek, and Knock

Ask and keep on asking and it shall be given you; seek and keep on seeking and you
shall find; knock and keep on knocking and the door shall be opened to you. For everyone
who asks and keeps on asking receives; and he who seeks and keeps on seeking finds;
and to him who knocks and keeps on knocking, the door shall be opened.
LUKE 11:9–10 AMPC

You have heard it from My lips. Ask and you will receive. But be persistent in that asking. Do not give up when the going looks impossible. For with Me, all things are possible. And follow up your asking with seeking. Do not just sit on your hands, but look, search, explore. Keep your mind and eyes open. For you will find Me working all around and within you.

And with your asking and seeking, continue to knock, to press, to lean on those doors of opportunity. Such continual efforts will be well rewarded. I have promised you. And as you know, I never lie.

Your side is to ask, seek, and knock. Mine is to answer, reveal, and open. Together, the seemingly impossible will become reality. Good things will be given. Dreams will be realized. And things will be set right as the will of Father God is done on earth as it is in heaven.

The Power of Harmony

*"The person who trusts me will not only do what I'm doing but even greater things,
because I, on my way to the Father, am giving you the same work to do that I've been
doing. You can count on it. From now on, whatever you request along the lines of who
I am and what I am doing, I'll do it. That's how the Father will be seen for who he
is in the Son. I mean it. Whatever you request in this way, I'll do."*
JOHN 14:12–14 MSG

Line up with My will and watch our combined power erupt into miracles!

Do not be like Jacob, who wrestled with God's will for his life. I do not want you limping around but walking tall. When you are aligned with Me, you will be a power to be reckoned with! For you will be in total harmony with the Father—just as humankind was supposed to be from the very beginning, from the creation of the world.

I came to earth to be your example, to save you from yourself, to reunite you with God, to get *His* vision for your life. So do not cloud your eyes with thoughts and desires that are not of God. Instead, set your sights on the tasks I have set before you, the continuation of the work I began— loving, caring, praying, communing with, and seeking Abba. Then I will do what you have asked.

Ask. Reach. Open.

We are not set right with God by rule-keeping but only through personal faith in Jesus Christ. . . .
Convinced that no human being can please God by self-improvement, we believed in Jesus as the
Messiah so that we might be set right before God by trusting in the Messiah, not by trying to be good.
GALATIANS 2:16 MSG

Rules, rules, rules. They will not save you. In fact, they will only stress you out even more. For there is no way you will be able to obey them all, keep them all, follow them all to perfection.

I am not asking for you to be perfect in every way. I am simply asking you to believe in Me. To have complete faith in Me being the Father's Son. To trust that I truly am the Way, the Life, and the Truth. To follow in My footsteps, the path I have laid out before you. That is the only way you and your ways and life will be made right with God.

Do you understand? If not, pray for such understanding. Make your seeking out and following Me the most important thing in your life. Speak to Me often, asking Me every little thing. I thrill at the sound of your voice. I long for the touch of your hand. I ache to share My life and light with you. So ask, reach, open. I am here, waiting to hear, connect, and fill.

Winning Favor

Obviously, I'm not trying to win the approval of people, but of God.
If pleasing people were my goal, I would not be Christ's servant.
GALATIANS 1:10 NLT

You are so busy seeking to win the favor of your fellow humans that you have forgotten to consult with Me. And now you are anxious, worried, spent, stressed, overwrought. For, as it turns out, and as you have learned time and time again, it is impossible to please people! Believe Me! I know! And when you try to please people, you will find yourself serving them instead of Abba God. You will be led down paths that you were not meant to walk. Your hands will be given tasks they were not meant to do. Your true vision will be blurred or, even worse, obstructed.

The remedy is to love others but not live to please them. Have the confidence to say no when you need to. Trust that My opinion and favor is of more value to you—in heaven and on earth. Have faith that I am the only one who can care for you, provide for you, unconditionally love you, prepare you, and lead you in the way you are to go. Pray; please only Me. Win My favor—and you will have the true victory!

Your Pathway

The steps of a [good] man are directed and established by the Lord when He delights in his way [and He busies Himself with his every step]. Though he falls, he shall not be utterly cast down, for the Lord grasps his hand in support and upholds him.
PSALM 37:23–24 AMPC

I not only tell you where and how to walk; I make the actual pathway on which you trod. Every moment of your life, I am watching. Every time you misstep, I reroute you. Even if you take a fall, I am there to reach out and grab your hand, help you to regain your balance and stand straight again.

Thus there is nowhere you can go that's out of My province. So look to Me for direction. Consult Me at every crossroads. Ask Me what lies ahead, and I will show you—because I have already gone ahead to check things out.

When you are walking in My will, My heart soars! I am thrilled with the possibilities, the opportunities that you will soon encounter. So ask Me every step of the way. As a sailor relies on the stars, you can rely on Me. I will help you navigate, even through the dark days of sorrow, grief, pain, and worry.

Peace be with you on the path I have provided.

Peace within His Order

For God is not a God of disorder but of peace.
1 CORINTHIANS 14:33 NIV

Tangled messes are My forte. Leave them in My hands.

The questions you cannot answer, the problems you cannot solve, the people you cannot abide, the circumstances you cannot control—these are all My province. So leave them at My feet. I will take them off your hands so that you will be free to do more important work—trusting Me and continuing to do what I have called you to do.

Ask the Holy Spirit to aid you in this endeavor, to support and strengthen you as you live this life with total trust that I will take care of everything. Ask for His counsel about what is to be worked on by you and what is to be left to Me. Home in on His voice. He will guide you to where you are to go, what you are to do. Where you do not find guidance wait for it, or leave things to Me.

In this way, you will find less strife and confusion in your life. This new avenue to order and peace will spark a new passion and vigor within you to tackle those things within your purview and to keep you on the path I have laid out before you.

Singing and Dancing

*Blessed (happy, fortunate, to be envied) are those who dwell in
Your house and Your presence; they will be singing Your praises
all the day long. Selah [pause, and calmly think of that]!*
PSALM 84:4 AMPC

I am the Lord of peace. I am the one in whose silence you may rest. I have stilled the waters of your heart before. I have calmed the wind of your distress as well. Here, with Me, you find the peace—the stillness—that the world so desperately craves.

So come to Me now. Do not delay! Seek My face. Rest against My chest. Allow no distressing thoughts to disturb you.

And do not just visit Me. Dwell with Me. Dwell within Me. Allow Me to surround you on every side, in every way. Look nowhere else but to Me. Remain here even when you go about your daily tasks. When you do, you will find an unsurpassed peace and joy. Others will see a radiance about you. They will want what you have—a thing that cannot be bought. Nor earned. A free gift from your Lord, sustainer, creator, maintainer.

In this way, you will not only be walking My way but showing others *the* Way. Prove Me in this. And you will find yourself singing My praises, dancing in My presence, all the day long.

Newfound Wisdom

Trust in the LORD with all your heart, and lean not on your own understanding;
in all your ways acknowledge Him, and He shall direct your paths.
PROVERBS 3:5–6 NKJV

———○◆◇———

I have formed you and the world you now live in. I have the knowledge of the ages—what has been, what is, and what will be. I am wisdom personified. I and My Word hold all the answers to the world's questions.

Your life presents many choices to you. Every day, decisions need to be made. Yet you look only to the world or to others in your life for the answers. Because of this you are often misled. Think on this. What questions, what decisions do you now have before you, in this very moment? What is troubling you? Now turn to Me in prayer. Look into My Word for wisdom. Then trust Me and the answers I provide. Only then ask for, reflect on, and test the counsel of others. If their advice is aligned with what I have shown you, it is sound.

When you are ready, move forward with your newfound wisdom. Know that I have set you on the right path. Rely on Me and My divine knowledge—not on your own limited understanding. Take heart. I have given you all the insight you need. Walk with courage. I am with you every step of the way. Acknowledge Me in this, and you will find the confidence to walk this path.

Empowered for Purpose

My response is to get down on my knees before the Father, this magnificent Father who parcels out all heaven and earth. I ask him to strengthen you by his Spirit—not a brute strength but a glorious inner strength—that Christ will live in you as you open the door and invite him in.
EPHESIANS 3:14–16 MSG

Over two thousand years ago, My followers were praying for you. Feel this truth deep within you. Believers have gone down on their knees, praying to our Abba God, asking Him to give you all the energy, power, strength of His Spirit—an amazing inner strength and light—to do what He has called you to do.

You have already invited Me to reside within you. And that is where I remain. See Me there. Feel the glow. Know that I am abiding within you, empowering you to live your purpose—to spend time with Me, to praise the Father, to allow the Spirit full reign, to love others as I have loved you. To look to helping others instead of merely helping yourself.

Let go of the angst, self-pity, and anxiety. Cling to the Father, Son, and Spirit. Absorb our strength, inner power, and wisdom. Trust that this is happening in this very moment. Feel the light, love, and hope that is surrounding you. Leave this place other-focused, as the little Christ you were called to be.

Lean on Me

Trust (lean on, rely on, and be confident) in the Lord and do good; so shall you
dwell in the land and feed surely on His faithfulness, and truly you shall be fed. . . .
Now there was leaning on Jesus' bosom one of His disciples, whom Jesus loved.
PSALM 37:3 AMPC, JOHN 13:23 NKJV

How I long to have you be that unnamed disciple, leaning back on Me, so relaxed in My company, hanging on to My every word. This is not a time for questions. This is a time for replenishing yourself with Me, making Me your food and water, becoming sated on My very presence.

When you trust in Me, you *expect* Me to hold you up. You can lean on Me without a care in the world, knowing I will support you. You rely on Me to meet every little need. You have the confidence that a young child has with her loving big brother, knowing he will provide, protect, and sacrifice his life for her.

And when you have such assurance in Me, such a calm manner when we sit together, you will have all your needs met. Cares and worries will drift away as you relax into My peace. And when you again arise, that peace will linger on as your day unfolds. For I walk with you.

Seek First

"What I'm trying to do here is get you to relax, not be so preoccupied with getting so you can respond to God's giving. People who don't know God and the way he works fuss over these things, but you know both God and how he works. Steep yourself in God-reality, God-initiative, God-provisions. You'll find all your everyday human concerns will be met. Don't be afraid of missing out. You're my dearest friends! The Father wants to give you the very kingdom itself."
LUKE 12:29–32 MSG

Seek Me and all that I am, and you will find everything that you need supplied!

Read My Word. Train yourself to see the world through My eyes. Trust that I am with you, I, the Lord of all creation. Be assured that nothing can touch you without first going through Me, that I will bend it to My will, and the result will be meant for your good. Believe that there is a plan, a wonderful plan. Envision a world where I light up the sky day and night. Where no tear will be shed, no pain felt, no loss realized.

Immerse yourself in that vision, knowing that I will take care of everything you could possibly desire, need, dream. You will want for nothing. In fact, when you make seeking God's way your first priority, He will give you the entire kingdom!

Mistakes

The godly may trip seven times, but they will get up again.
But one disaster is enough to overthrow the wicked.
PROVERBS 24:16 NLT

Every mistake you make is a learning opportunity. So do not mourn or fret or become anxious about your error. Instead, rise up after you trip up. Make the most of your blunder by learning from it. Take note of what made you stumble. Ask Me for guidance, help, wisdom, and light for your feet. Factor into your life things that will make your path smoother. Once you are again upright, standing, practice the good way and hope for the best. Know that I am with you, holding you by the hand, sending angels to help you on your way.

Whatever you do, don't give up. Instead, keep going, hoping for another opportunity to become better, wiser, closer to Me. In doing so, you will learn how to endure, how to persevere, how to keep trusting in Me every step of the way. How to have joy in any situation.

And before you know it, you will find yourself standing taller in your faith.

Dear brothers and sisters, when troubles of any kind come your way, consider it an opportunity
for great joy. For you know that when your faith is tested, your endurance has a chance to grow.
JAMES 1:2–3 NLT

The Joy of Believing

Sarah laughed within herself, saying, "After I have grown old, shall I have pleasure,
my lord being old also?" And the LORD said to Abraham, "Why did Sarah laugh,
saying, 'Shall I surely bear a child, since I am old?' Is anything too hard for the LORD?"
. . . Abraham was one hundred years old when his son Isaac was born to him.
And Sarah said, "God has made me laugh, and all who hear will laugh with me."
GENESIS 18:12–14; 21:5–6 NKJV

There are two types of laughter in My Word—the negative laughter of disbelief and the positive laughter of the believer. Sarah practiced both.

When the elderly Sarah heard she was going to give birth to Abraham's son in the very near future, she laughed with unbelief! And then, when our Father confronted her about it, she, in fear, denied doing so! Yet when provision was made, when the prediction, the promise, became a reality, only then did she laugh with the true joy of believing!

If only you would live your life as a true believer, knowing that what I have promised is already a reality in your life. Then you would not live fearing or fretting but as a joyful follower of the One whose word is your very life.

Think on these things. Believe that there is nothing too hard for the One who parted seas, rose from the dead, walked among the living, and now resides in you.

Early Morning Hours

Before daybreak the next morning, Jesus got up and went out to an
isolated place to pray. Later Simon and the others went out to find him.
MARK 1:35–36 NLT

In these early morning hours, lie still. Lie still before Me until you feel My presence approach and lie down by your side.

Let us then lie together in companionable silence where peace and contentment—Mine and yours—reign and abide, within and without. The demands of the world fade away. The hammering of life becomes a dim memory. The sounds of the birds a sweet refrain. The whoosh of wind a harmless echo. And then there is left amid our silence the comfort of the love we share, the hope we cherish, the peace we crave, alone together, in the Father's arms, cradled until it is time to rise together, remade, redeemed, and recharged, to go about our Father's business.

Treasure these moments. For they are but a prelude to a day we will face together, a day in which you are filled with calm, courage, and confidence. A day in which you need not worry about your strength or power, but merely allow Me to continue on with you, to work through you, in you, and with you. A day in which mountains will be moved and trees uprooted.

God Pays Attention

*"What's the price of two or three pet canaries? Some loose change, right? But God
never overlooks a single one. And he pays even greater attention to you,
down to the last detail—even numbering the hairs on your head!"*
LUKE 12:6–7 MSG

I am interested in every little thing. Each breath that you take. The pulse of your lifeblood. The hairs on your head. The pent-up sigh you set free. Each and every concern that you have, thought in your mind, word upon your lips. Each has a source, a beginning point. And each has an end.

Give Me every frown, doubt, worry, laugh, song, sob, praise, and prayer. Be faithful in coming to me with all these little things. And your reward will be, in this divine sharing, a freedom that is found nowhere else. For only I am equipped to carry your load. Only My shoulders can bear the weight of what you are trying to carry.

So in this moment, relax. Let down your guard. Stop fighting to keep what can only bring you down. Hand it over to Me. For only I can set you free. Only I can make all things—even the tiniest of worms or germs—work out for your supreme good. For I truly doeth and maketh all things well.

All Is Well

Fret not yourself because of evildoers, neither be envious against those who work unrighteousness (that which is not upright or in right standing with God). For they shall soon be cut down like the grass, and wither as the green herb. . . . Wait for and expect the Lord and keep and heed His way, and He will exalt you to inherit the land; [in the end] when the wicked are cut off, you shall see it.
PSALM 37:1–2, 34 AMPC

Those who have not yet heard or wanted My message of love can cause chaos in My otherwise orderly world—and yours, as well. In those times, worldly what-ifs that careen around in your mind can cause you to lose your balance.

Yet I tell you, do not be dismayed at those who are not walking in the Way. Do not allow them to disrupt your purpose, your calling, your expectations. For that will only hinder your way or misdirect you from the paths I have laid out for you.

Instead, leave all to Me. I am watching. I know each person's path and purpose. Everyone will receive their due in time. It is not for you to worry about or focus on.

Simply wait for Me to work. Watch for Me, expect Me, know that your end will be well. Let that content you. For now, that's all you need to know. All is well. And all will be well.

Walking with Courage and Ease

For the Lord God is a Sun and Shield; the Lord bestows [present] grace
and favor and [future] glory (honor, splendor, and heavenly bliss)!
No good thing will He withhold from those who walk uprightly.
PSALM 84:11 AMPC

———◦•◦———

You moan over the past, are anxious in the present, and fear the future. But this should not be!

Walk closer to Me. In doing so, you will find that I am the bright light that shines in every area of your life! Nothing is hidden from Me or My power. I am your enlightener and protector. No foe can withstand My strength.

And this is not just for this present moment. This encompasses your past, your present, and your future. I have erased your past. Let it fall away, out of your thoughts. I am building your future, filling it with things that will bring you joy, hope, and promise. But more important than those two, I am in your present. Here I have given you all that you need to make the most and the best of this life you have been gifted. Here you stand forgiven and blessed.

So allow your regrets, worries, and fears to be banished by My light. Walk forward with courage and ease, knowing I am guarding you in each and every situation. Honor Me in this.

Far beyond Imagination

Now to Him Who, by (in consequence of) the [action of His] power that is at work within us, is able to [carry out His purpose and] do superabundantly, far over and above all that we [dare] ask or think [infinitely beyond our highest prayers, desires, thoughts, hopes, or dreams]—to Him be glory.
EPHESIANS 3:20–21 AMPC

You have an amazing power deep within you, continually working. It does not sleep when you lie down for the night. It does not grow ill when your body sickens.

No. This power needs neither sleep nor remedies. It is Me working within you, gently, deeply, constantly. Live in the fullness that this power gives you. Know that this power is endeavoring to carry out God's purposes so far beyond what you ever hoped or imagined!

Do not hesitate to remember this power every moment of every day. With this in mind, you know that nothing anyone says or does can hurt you. There is no situation you cannot rise above. No problem you cannot surmount. No conflict you cannot conquer. No temptation you cannot escape from.

With Me living within you, challenges become opportunities, problems become stepping-stones, and enemies become friends. Understand this. And let this understanding absolve your anxieties, power your passion, and charge your courage. With such power, there is nothing we cannot do together.

Walk through the Next Door

*"This is the message from the one who is holy and true, the one who has the key
of David. What he opens, no one can close; and what he closes, no one can open:
I know all the things you do, and I have opened a door for you that no one can close."*

REVELATION 3:7–8 NLT

I have called you to do a certain task, to follow a specific calling. Yet you do not move for fear you are making or will make a mistake. Here is where your faith—in Me and yourself as well—is crucial to your (and My) progress.

Trust Me in all the paths to which I lead you. Know that I have supplied all that you need to answer that calling. Trust that I am walking with you, that you will find a new passion and joy within this venture.

You may not yet see the entire picture, but I do. I know exactly where you are now, where you are heading, what you will learn on the way, and what you will accomplish at the end.

So do not worry. Simply take My hand and walk through the next door I have opened for you. Move forward in confidence and hope, believing not only in Me but in the Father and the Holy Spirit who move with you.

Love Is All Around

*"Let me give you a new command: Love one another. In the same way I loved you,
you love one another. This is how everyone will recognize that you are
my disciples—when they see the love you have for each other."*
JOHN 13:34–35 MSG

Love is all around you—for God is love. So look for love. Open yourself to receive love. Determine to give love.

Spend much time in My presence. For it is there that you will learn about how to love, how much it has to offer you, how much the world yearns for it. Love is like water in a dry and thirsty land. People ache for a kind word, a gentle touch, a nod of acknowledgment, a silent smile, a listening ear, a hug of compassion, a glance of understanding. These all seem like such little things. Yet these little things mean so much more to a soul and spirit bereft of love.

And once you begin looking for love, signs of love will pop up all around you, amazing you, giving you joy, fueling your sense of expectation. This is Me, reminding you that I am never far. Merely a breath away.

Follow My command to love one another. And you will find, as you turn your focus from self to others, that all your worries fade away, dissipate like a low-hanging fog that meets the sun's first rays.

An Inner Knowing

As you know not what is the way of the wind, or how the
spirit comes to the bones in the womb of a pregnant woman,
even so you know not the work of God, Who does all.
ECCLESIASTES 11:5 AMPC

There are many mysteries to which you are not privy. But do not let that make you uneasy. You don't need to know all things, to have all the answers.

Remember that I have and hold the vision for your life. Although I do grant you some sight, I do not give you the entire picture. So rest in the knowledge that I do hold all the answers. That I am *the* answer, *the* artist, *the* author.

And although My thoughts are so much higher than your thoughts, I *do* give you all the light you need to find your way, all the insight you require to fulfill your purpose, all the talent necessary to pursue your calling.

Rest assured that you are a part of the grand plan, a necessary piece of the tapestry I am creating, weaving, strand by strand. So do not turn aside from your path, but trod it with an inner knowing that you will be able to accomplish all I have created, prepared, and trained you for, one task, one step, one stitch at a time.

Following in His Footsteps

Righteousness will go before Him,
and shall make His footsteps our pathway.
PSALM 85:13 NKJV

I see that you are at a standstill. That you do not know what is the next step for you. At this point—and any other point in which you are anxious or have any doubts or are uncertain about which way to go—follow Me.

You know Me. You have read the accounts of witnesses of Me. You have heard My stories, My history, My songs time and time again. Take these words to heart. Learn who I am.

I am the one that loved the woman at the well, the woman with the flow of blood, the man who doubted I could heal his son, the followers who fled when I was arrested. I healed the lame, gave sight to the blind, cleaned the skin of the leper. I forgave those who beat, whipped, and hung Me until the last breath left My body.

In My life on earth, I obeyed My Father. I sought places where I could be alone and spend precious moments in His presence. I yearned for this. For it was those moments of replenishment that gave Me the power to love, to have compassion, to heal, preach, and teach.

This is the lesson: Follow in My footsteps. Love and forgive without being loved and forgiven by others in return. There is nothing I would not do for you. So do all for Me.

Master Knitter

*Through him all things were made; without him nothing was made that
has been made. In him was life, and that life was the light of all mankind.*

JOHN 1:3–4 NIV

———◦•◦———

Too long away from time in My presence and you begin to unravel. Remember that I am the one that knit you together. I know exactly how you were made—for I created you! When you were deep within the body of another, just a seed of life, My hands formed every part of your being—body, spirit, mind, and soul. Before you took a breath or felt the sun upon your face, I was filling your lungs and growing you in the darkness. When you were a mere babe, I protected you and gave you all you needed to stand where you are today.

I am the one who grows, replenishes, strengthens, feeds, tends, cares for you. Do not neglect the source of power you have when you abide with Me, in Me. Do not forsake the master knitter, the craftsman who knows you better than anyone in the world.

Come to Me each day—in sorrow, angst, joy, relief, anger, heartache, forgiveness, confusion, peace. Whatever mode or mood you are in, seek Me. And in doing so, you will find the Light that leads you to not only well-being but triumph—in heaven and on earth.

*For you created my inmost being;
you knit me together in my mother's womb.*

PSALM 139:13 NIV

Fruitful Promises

So shall My word be that goes forth out of My mouth: it shall not return to Me void [without producing any effect, useless], but it shall accomplish that which I please and purpose, and it shall prosper in the thing for which I sent it.
ISAIAH 55:11 AMPC

My Word is filled with promises to you. I promise never to leave or forsake you. I promise to give you direction, insight, and wisdom. I promise that everything that happens to you will be for your good. I promise that if you obey Me, your life will be blessed. I promise you peace, joy, and eternal life. I promise you the gift of the Holy Spirit, one that is sent to all who believe.

Know that every promise that I make in the Word, every word of truth that I speak into your ear, has power. It will produce fruit; it will prosper—wherever I send it, wherever it is heard. My promises will give you courage, steadiness, hope, encouragement, wisdom, strength, and vision. And your belief in them will give you the power to do the impossible.

So in time when you are in despair, fearful, or anxious, claim My promises. Know they will prosper you. Rest on their power. Realize their purpose. And expect them to bear fruit.

But the fruit of the Spirit is love, joy, peace, longsuffering, kindness, goodness, faithfulness, gentleness, self-control. Against such there is no law.
GALATIANS 5:22–23 NKJV

The True Savior

*GOD, the Master, The Holy of Israel, has this solemn counsel: "Your salvation requires
you to turn back to me and stop your silly efforts to save yourselves. Your strength will come
from settling down in complete dependence on me— the very thing you've been unwilling to do."*
ISAIAH 30:15 MSG

So many things are vying for your attention, offered as the cure, the answer, the miracle. But none of these can save you. Only I can do that.

So come back to Me. Return to Me. Rest in Me. There, within Me, does your strength lie. I am the only one who can give you confidence to do what you have been called to do. You know this, yet you continue to rely on everything *but* Me!

There is no way you can accomplish what I have already done—and am *still doing*—for you. Take a moment to let this sink in. Consider it a fact, a solemn truth. Can a drowning person save herself? No. That person needs a calm, strong, and well-trained lifeguard to take hold of and pull her safely to shore.

I am that lifeguard. So stop flailing, trying to save yourself. Relax in Me. Float upon the troubled waters of your life. Allow Me to get a firm grip and pull you safely to shore. Trust in no one and nothing but Me—for I am the only true Savior in this world and the next.

Joys in Life

O Lord of hosts, blessed (happy, fortunate, to be envied) is the man
who trusts in You [leaning and believing on You, committing all and
confidently looking to You, and that without fear or misgiving]!
PSALM 84:12 AMPC

All the joys in life are wrapped up in the knowledge that all has been committed to and taken care of by Me, whether those concerns are from the past, in the present, or toward the future.

This you know. Yet still there are times when some of your worries are turned over to Me. But others you cling to, grip with white knuckles, certain that you'll find your way out.

This should not be. This proves that you do not trust Me with all. That you think you'll find a better answer than I have already planned to provide you. You are blocking My way by holding on to a concern that was not for you to carry to begin with.

Trust ALL in Me! Put all your fears and doubts behind you. Do it every time the wrong thoughts and emotions surround you. Say, "Jesus, come to me now!" or "Jesus, give me peace," or even just, "Jesus," and I will immediately respond. I will save you from what threatens to harm and hinder you. I have already saved you once. Allow Me, use Me, to give you confidence, to live a life of joy in Me.

Under Control

"I, your GOD, have a firm grip on you and I'm not letting go. I'm telling you,
'Don't panic. I'm right here to help you.' Do you feel like a lowly worm, Jacob?
Don't be afraid. . . . I'll help you. I, GOD, want to reassure you."
ISAIAH 41:13–14 MSG

"God has got it under control. God has got it all under control." Plant those words firmly in your mind. Let them take root there. And when they do—when they have become strong and sturdy, a part of your very fabric and being—your cares will ebb away.

The knowledge that I have things in hand—including you—will keep you from leaking energy in other areas of your life, areas in which you need to be strong so that you can do what you have been called to do. Knowing I have things under control will keep your focus on Me, not your problems.

If you are worried about finances, your job, your home, your government, do not despair. Simply envision Me, My firm grip on you. Hear Me tell you not to worry, run, hide, fret, or panic. I'm right here with you, every step of the way. This is My message, My reassurance, My good word, My promise to you. Believe it. Live it. And leave your anxiety behind.

But a Child

*Truly I say to you, unless you repent (change, turn about) and become like little children
[trusting, lowly, loving, forgiving], you can never enter the kingdom of heaven [at all].
Whoever will humble himself therefore and become like this little child [trusting,
lowly, loving, forgiving] is greatest in the kingdom of heaven.*
MATTHEW 18:3–4 AMPC

In My eyes, you are but a child. For I have existed since before time. I am the Son of the Ancient of Days. So come to us as a child, expecting the protection, love, provision, and forgiveness every child expects from its parent. Believe with your entire being. Be wide-eyed at the marvelous things I am going to do in your life.

When you are frightened, run to Me, jump into My arms, knowing that here nothing can harm you. When you are unsure, come to Me for advice, knowing I have the answers. When you are anxious, find in Me the peace and assurance that everything I have is yours. You need simply ask and I will provide.

And as a child mimics its parents, mimic Me. Follow in My footsteps. For as you do so, I will give you all you need to do even more than I did while walking on the earth. And open to you will be the kingdom of heaven.

Secret Prayers Openly Rewarded

But when you pray, go into your [most] private room, and, closing
the door, pray to your Father, Who is in secret; and your Father,
Who sees in secret, will reward you in the open.
MATTHEW 6:6 AMPC

You seek Me, your heart in your hand, looking for relief from the issues of the past, the pressures of the day, the questions of the night, the worries of the future. Quietly come to Me in your secret place, where we can together commune in silence. Close the door behind you. Let no person, thought, doubt, or misgiving enter here. Speak to Me of your troubles away from the crowd. Pray to Me in this secret place. When you do so, your Father God, your Abba, will reward you.

The answer you seek may or may not be yours. Sometimes a loss to you is actually a gain, although you do not yet see it. If My followers had not lost Me, they would not have been given the gift of the Holy Spirit.

All is not always as it seems. That is why you must trust Me to make all things right.

Pray to Me in secret. Fast in secret. Give to others in secret. Your Father is watching you and will reward you in the open. This is His way. This is His promise.

Peace from Spirit to Spirit

I will listen [with expectancy] to what God the Lord will say, for He
will speak peace to His people, to His saints (those who are in right
standing with Him)— but let them not turn again to [self-confident] folly.
PSALM 85:8 AMPC

You come to Me with your prayers. You have emptied out your heart, told Me all, the supposed good as well as the bad. You have unburdened yourself as I have asked you to do.

Now wait. Listen. Hear what I have to say. Know that I will speak. My words, although they may not be exactly what you want to hear, will give you peace. They will lift up your spirit. They will give you a sense of hope, an expectation of the good things that are already in and are about to come into your life.

Yet the peace that this conversation, this speaking and listening on both sides, provides will have no staying power if you leave this place and go back to depending on yourself to meet all needs, answer all questions.

So make a fresh start. Leave your self-reliance in the dust. Stick with Me, totally depending on Me alone. And you will have the peace you so crave, the peace that brings joy, understanding, and well-being. The awesome, all-encompassing peace of God, given from Spirit to spirit.

A Friend for Eternity

There is a friend who sticks closer than a brother.
PROVERBS 18:24 NKJV

⸺◦◆◦⸺

I will never leave you or abandon you. That is My promise, one that I make over and over again to all, although they may be hesitant to believe.

My own disciples made this I-will-never-leave-you promise to Me, but in the end, when events became very difficult, all but one deserted Me. I know this is often the way of humankind, but that does not make it any easier, nor any less painful.

You may have felt as if you were left behind in times past. This makes it hard for you to trust Me. But that's exactly what I ask you to do. Trust Me. Know that the promise of My presence in your life, through thick and thin, is something you can count on.

My Father never abandoned Joseph while he was sold, enslaved, unjustly accused, wrongly imprisoned, and forgotten. But through all that, Joseph was never alone, never without My Father's companionship; and because Joseph knew and believed this, he ended up prospering beyond belief.

I do what My Father does. Thus, rest assured that no matter what is happening in your life, I will always be with you, encouraging, strengthening, empowering, loving, holding, provisioning, molding, and prospering. Never doubt that in Me you have a friend for eternity.

Not Shaken

I will bless the LORD who guides me; even at night my heart instructs me.
I know the LORD is always with me. I will not be shaken, for he is right beside me.
PSALM 16:7–8 NLT

When you are in tune with Me, seeking My Word, My counsel, your heart is more at peace. But when you neglect to include Me in your life, when you step away from your time in My presence, you may find yourself experiencing sleepless nights.

May this not be so! When you are awake, come to Me. Question Me. Ask Me for direction, help, advice. Allow Me to guide you through this life, to help you navigate around the reefs, amid the storms, against the tidal waves. I am the One who can carry you over the reefs, still the storms, and calm the waves—no matter what time of the day or night.

Be confident that I am with you always, a constant presence in your life. That I am right beside you. Stick with Me as I stick with you. Cling to Me as I cling to you. Then you will be standing on solid rock. Then nothing will shake you. Then you will sleep in perfect peace for your heart, soul, body, mind, and spirit have been touched, buoyed by My Spirit and light.

In Step

Whether the cloud stayed above the Tabernacle for two days, a month, or a year,
the people of Israel stayed in camp and did not move on. But as soon as it lifted,
they broke camp and moved on. So they camped or traveled at the Lord's
command, and they did whatever the Lord told them through Moses.

NUMBERS 9:22–23 NLT

What peace there is for those who are in step with Me. What faith those have who look to Me for every direction.

You seek Me to unburden your heart but then at times do not wait for a response. Then you misstep and wonder why I didn't warn you.

Be as the people of God, wandering in the wilderness. Seek Me for all things. Wait upon My answer. Do not move out or change direction or stop until you are sure of My guidance. When I say it is time to move out, to change tack, do not delay. When I say it is time to stop, to rest, to wait, do so. Look to Me. Rest with Me. Follow Me. Wait with Me. All the while, be confident that I am watching, that I have the divine timing, and that I am doing what is best for you. I am leading you through the wilderness, intent on guiding you safely into your Promised Land.

Ever Closer

So then, whatever you desire that others would do to and for you, even so
do also to and for them, for this is (sums up) the Law and the Prophets.
MATTHEW 7:12 AMPC

How simple the life of you, My follower, would be if you simply treated others how you want to be treated. And did for others what they would like to have done for them. For this is what it is all about. This is what I have done for you.

If you lived every minute of your day with the ancient command to do unto others as you would have them do unto you in the forefront of your mind, at the center of your heart, and left everything else up to Me, how worry free your life would be! How at peace your mind. And what seeds you would plant, what fruit you would reap! What treasures you would store up in heaven!

Living such a life, you would be deemed not only a believer in, but a doer of My words of love, one that others would look to for compassion, help, forgiveness, mercy, a listening ear. You would be one that others look at and find Me shining through.

Take one step closer today to embodying this command. Write it upon your heart. Embed it in your mind. And we will draw ever closer.

Joy and Contentment

Be happy [in your faith] and rejoice and be glad-hearted continually (always); be unceasing in prayer [praying perseveringly].
1 Thessalonians 5:16–17 AMPC

The resource of prayer. Never forget its amazing and unyielding power to change anything and everything it touches.

Incessantly come before Me, sharing every little thing. Make it a continual conversation. Tell Me how you feel, what you're doing, what you hope for, the desired outcome of all your encounters and endeavors.

Amid your petitions, sprinkle praise, spice things up with gratitude. All this will give you a new awareness of My presence in the everyday minutiae and the big moments as well. It will also keep you looking for all the things I am already doing in your life for which you are grateful. All those everyday blessings you may be taking for granted.

This continual praying and praising will keep you in the right state of mind, body, soul, and spirit, leaving little room for anxieties and fears. It will become not only an ever-thickening and strengthening bond between your spirit and Mine but an addictive and inspiring source of joy and contentment.

Prove Me in this. And you will find yourself becoming more and more the person We created you to be, connected to and melding ever further into Father God and Me.

Find the Blessing

Thank [God] in everything [no matter what the circumstances may be, be thankful and give thanks], for this is the will of God for you [who are] in Christ Jesus [the Revealer and Mediator of that will] . . . . But test and prove all things [until you can recognize] what is good; [to that] hold fast.

1 Thessalonians 5:18, 21 AMPC

———◁◆▷———

Know that I am the Lord over all these things. I have the power to make and unmake. All is in My hands—including you! I am Lord of the "takes" and "mistakes," using, working with all to come out for good.

So do not despair or fear. I am filtering all things, reshaping, repurposing, reforming all to adapt to My master plan for creation.

What is seemingly used against you, I will rework for your good. Be content with this knowledge, filled with wonder, gratitude, and praise. I will one day reveal all to you. For now, see all as a good thing, a thing I am working on. Leave it in My hands. Have the expectation that no matter how things look today, there *will* be a better day tomorrow.

Step back. Gain My perspective. And see My hand in all things. And in all things you will find the blessing and give Me praise.

Watch. Wait.

"Blessed are those who listen to me, watching daily at my doors, waiting at my doorway. For those who find me find life and receive favor from the LORD."
PROVERBS 8:34–35 NIV

You are so diverted and distraught by worldly events. You are waylaid by slights from others and weighed down by your own missteps. All these things don't just keep you from doing your kingdom work. They keep you distracted while in—or completely away from—My presence.

The remedy is to spend quality time with Me. Go to My Word and read the things I have said to My followers, the words that came directly from My very lips. Make them part of your very consciousness. Live and breathe them until they are a part of your core, your solid foundation. Embed My words in your mind so that when darts of doubt arise, you have a shield of faith to protect you from all misgivings.

You are My hands, feet, heart, and mouthpiece. Become strong. Stand for Me. Love others beyond measure. Look for Me in all. Come to Me now. Stand at My doorway, your heart in hand. Enter into My presence. Drift back into Me. Get ready to listen, to receive, then watch. Wait. I will do the rest. I will tell you all.

A Marvelous Day

This is from the Lord and is His doing; it is marvelous in our eyes. This is the
day which the Lord has brought about; we will rejoice and be glad in it.
PSALM 118:23–24 AMPC

Thank Me for this day. May it be one in which My light shines through you. One in which you are a conduit of My love, joy, grace, mercy, and forgiveness—to not only others but yourself as well.

This day is in My hands. It is all My doing. Take it as such. Celebrate it as such. Do not allow the day's events to shake you. Instead, when a challenge arises, look to Me and ask, "Yes, Lord? What would You have me do here? What would You have me say?" Then listen. When you have gotten a response, do not delay to carry out the task, to speak the words I have assigned.

Expect wonderful things to be seen, heard, revealed. Look for My hand in all. Trust that I am with you every step of the way.

Look to help those to whom I guide you. On this and every day you are able, seek to show love to someone you encounter upon your pathway. Even if it's only a smile, a nod of recognition, an understanding response, lead with compassion. Make this day I have given you not only a gift for yourself but marvelous in the eyes of another, one at the end of which you may both rejoice.

Constant Peace

You will guard him and keep him in perfect and constant peace
whose mind [both its inclination and its character] is stayed on You,
because he commits himself to You, leans on You, and hopes confidently in You.
ISAIAH 26:3 AMPC

Walk with Me. Spend time resting in Me. Continue to meet with Me during some part of your day be it ever so little. For like anyone whom you might cease spending time with, you will grow apart from Me. And soon, other things will take precedence. Soon I would begin to fade away from your awareness. That is when you might begin to feel seemingly inescapable turmoil creeping into your life.

But if you guard your time with Me, I will guard you as well—mind, body, heart, soul, and spirit. Because you commit yourself to Me, you will find peace a constant part of your life. When you lean on Me, coming to Me with every worry, heartache, question, sorrow, and doubt, peace cannot help but prevail. For I will give you the wisdom of God, His supernatural strength and power, and unwavering love.

Hope in Me. Know that what I have promised is yours. Know that I hold the vision for your life. Know that I hold the key to what is seen and unseen. And know that in all this lies the un-fathomable and constant peace your confidence in Me brings into your life.

Your Desired Destination

A strong wind was blowing and the waters grew rough. When they had rowed about three
or four miles, they saw Jesus approaching the boat. . . . Then they were willing to take him
into the boat, and immediately the boat reached the shore where they were heading.
JOHN 6:18–19, 21 NIV

Know that I am praying for you. I witness all that is happening in your life. I see you as I once did My disciples, struggling amid the storm-tossed waves, rowing, straining, striving in all your own efforts to reach the shore. Yet this should not be. Do you not see Me? I am walking through that storm, approaching you in the darkness that surrounds you.

When you see a glimpse of Me, do not be terrified. Know, recognize, that *I* am the one who can save you—if you would just invite Me into your craft, into your life, into your storm.

Do not be frightened. But be willing to take Me in. For as soon as you do, that peace that only I can provide will overwhelm you, suffuse you. The storm that once tortured you will abate. The wind and the waves will cease. You will be filled with heavenly gladness. And, immediately, you will glide through the sea of your life and reach your desired destination—no matter where you are or where you are headed.

Mighty Warrior

*When the angel of the Lord appeared to Gideon, he said, "The Lord is
with you, mighty warrior." . . . Then the Spirit of the Lord came on Gideon.*
Judges 6:12, 34 NIV

———◦◆◦———

I already see you as you were created to be. I know you as a mighty follower of much courage. Like Gideon, you might try to convince Me that you are the poorest and least of your people. But I know better. I see better. When I look at you, I see the vision of who you are becoming.

So take heart. I am here, sitting under the tree, casually watching you, letting you know that you are more than you think you are—especially with Me close by your side. So claim your power and confidence. I am sending you out and I will be with you, right by your side in all your encounters and circumstances. Be calm in your going. Exude the supernatural peace that I make available to you in abundance and that others so dearly crave.

Know that I will clothe you with Myself—all the armor you need to meet all challengers. Be assured that victory is in your hand. When I am with you, how could it be otherwise?

Walk in the power I have bestowed upon you. You are My fearless, peace-exuding, mighty warrior. A force to be reckoned with. Go forward in this truth.

Such Great Faith

Then Jesus turned to the captain and said, "Go. What you believed
could happen has happened." At that moment his servant became well.
MATTHEW 8:13 MSG

Your thoughts, mind-set, and attitude have everything to do with how much of My power appears in your life. Has this not been proven? Was there not so much disbelief in My own hometown that I could do nothing but heal a few ailing bodies?

Test your thoughts. Look deep within. Do not limit My hand by having no true faith, a surface faith at best.

Instead, follow the lead of the woman who had the flow of blood. She *knew* that I could heal her. She kept repeating that thought to herself until she reached out. I actually felt My power leaving Me—and she was healed immediately.

Believe as the leper who knew for a fact that if I was willing, I could make him clean. Believe as the centurion who, in looking for Me to heal his servant, demonstrated such great faith that I said, "Be on your way. As you have believed, so will it be done for you"—and his servant was healed within that hour.

Do not waste the power that is readily available to you by thinking anxious thoughts, thoughts of doom and gloom. Instead, believe that I am taking care of you. I am working within you. I will never leave you. Then watch Me prove it by the power I supply.

That Next Path

That's why we live with such good cheer. You won't see us drooping our heads or dragging our feet! Cramped conditions here don't get us down. They only remind us of the spacious living conditions ahead. It's what we trust in but don't yet see that keeps us going.

2 CORINTHIANS 5:6–7 MSG

Why are you so stressed out over the woulda, shoulda, couldas? Why are you letting your worries get you down?

I am the Lord of new things! I bring you out of the darkness and into the light! I am doing so now! So don't let where you are keep you from getting to where I am sending you. Know that amazing things, things you cannot yet see, lie just around the corner.

For now, just stand firm in your faith, knowing I can do the impossible—if you will only believe! Be alert for where I am working. Keep trusting that I have a better plan for your life. Watch for the clues I am giving you along the way, ones that will lead you down that next path. In doing so, you will grow in faith and My power will increase in your life. If you refuse to be tripped up and held back by your doubts, if you will only believe in Me with your entire mind, heart, body, and soul, nothing in heaven or on earth will be impossible for you.

A Perfect Peaceableness

And He said to them, Why are you timid and afraid, O you of little faith?
Then He got up and rebuked the winds and the sea, and there was
a great and wonderful calm (a perfect peaceableness).
MATTHEW 8:26 AMPC

———◦•◦———

You willingly follow Me, step by step. But as soon as a challenge arises or a storm creeps up, as soon as there is a testing period that rocks your world, you panic. You wonder where I am. Perhaps you even imagine I am sleeping. Otherwise how would this have happened to you?

You ask, "Where are You, Lord? Do You not see what is happening? Why don't You rescue me?"

Hang on. Gird up your faith. Know that I am with you in all things. And know this: I do have power over the wind and waves. And I can keep your world from rocking. But it all begins by stilling the storm within you. I work from the inside out.

Begin by believing this truth: The path to perfect peaceableness starts with calming your mind, heart, and spirit. By taking deep breaths and walking with Me in the green pastures and beside the quiet waters. Once you have that inner calm, then and only then will your outer world by extension become to you a place of stillness.

Bearing Up

You have seen what I did to the Egyptians, and how
I bore you on eagles' wings and brought you to Myself.
EXODUS 19:4 AMPC

History has shown you, time and time again, how I work, how I rescue those who love Me.

So do not let your feathers be ruffled. Know that I can take you out of any situation—or help you find a way to bear up underneath it. For at times I stir up your nest so that you can try out your wings, take on challenges, test your mettle. Yet if at any time during that testing you need help, I will swoop into the situation at your first cry. Together we can rise up above your worries, your concerns. From that height, all will be put into perspective. Your heart will calm, your confidence will be replenished, and your spirit will soar. For you are with Me, the one who lifts you above the earth when you lose your footing.

Follow Me as an eaglet follows its mother, discovering how to not only survive but flourish to the fullest. And know that, when the going gets tough, I will bear you up on My own wings and bring you to Myself.

As an eagle that stirs up her nest, that flutters over her young, He spread
abroad His wings and He took them, He bore them on His pinions.
DEUTERONOMY 32:11 AMPC

A Life Revived

Turn away my eyes from looking at worthless things, and revive me in Your way. . . . I will never forget Your precepts, for by them You have given me life.
PSALM 119:37, 93 NKJV

The more time you spend with Me, the more you grow to know Me—and the newer your life becomes each and every day. You will become wiser, for you will know what I would have you do. And when you obey My precepts, My commandments, when you do what I would have you do whether you understand it or not and without question, you will find yourself living in a whole new and spectacular world!

Be like a child on her father's knees, obeying Me because I say so. Choose a life of faithfulness. Cling to what I have told you. Be a part of My story. Live from a God-perspective. Walk within the light that I bring into every nook and cranny of your existence. Meditate on what I have told you. Bathe yourself in the Word. And you will begin to see all things through My eyes. Worry will vanish. Misgivings dissipate. Moments of panic disappear.

In this new life, a life revived by the power and Spirit of God, nothing but peace, confidence, courage, and hope will prevail. For I will be at the heart of it—and you.

A Wonder-Filled Day

*My child, eat honey, for it is good, and the honeycomb is sweet to
the taste. In the same way, wisdom is sweet to your soul. If you find it,
you will have a bright future, and your hopes will not be cut short.*
PROVERBS 24:13–14 NLT

I have in My hand not only your todays but your tomorrows as well. So do not despair over your future, do not agonize over what may happen in the days ahead. Instead, focus your energy and thoughts on today and the task I have brought to your hand.

This is how you have been made, to only concern yourself with the moment before you. Leave all else in My hands. In this way, you will have peace of mind and heart. And you will be a better and more creative laborer for Me and My kingdom. You will be freed up to see possibilities that you never glimpsed before. Your hopes and dreams will acquire a freshness brought about by the new ease you feel.

Relax. I've got everything under control. Know that I have already gone before you and cleared your pathway. Allow this new wisdom to reenergize you, to keep you moving forward and making progress in the Way. Seek the blessings of this moment, confident of a bright and hope-filled to-morrow. Have an amazing and wonder-filled day.

Intimate with the Father

*By faith, Noah built a ship in the middle of dry land. He was warned about
something he couldn't see, and acted on what he was told. The result? His family
was saved. His act of faith drew a sharp line between the evil of the unbelieving world
and the rightness of the believing world. As a result, Noah became intimate with God.*
HEBREWS 11:7 MSG

See Me. Believe Me. Know Me. I will show you the God-reality, the life, the Way, the truth that will lead you above a world of worries.

The world sees things differently. It may deem you foolish. But yet you are the wise one. Because you believe in those things that I have told you and act on what I have said—whether or not it makes sense to you—you will be saved.

Walk so closely with Me that you become intimate with the Father. Let faith be your motivator, prompting you to live the life I have called you to live. Let faith be your compass, your guide to the true path. Let faith conduct you to the true purpose for which you were created and designed. Such great faith will be tested on God's waters and be found not wanting.

Take Heart

He was despised and rejected—a man of sorrows, acquainted with deepest grief. . . .
Yet it was our weaknesses he carried; it was our sorrows that weighed him down.
ISAIAH 53:3–4 NLT

Let Me be the one who comforts you when you are broken over the loss of a loved one. I am acquainted with sorrow. And I am here to carry your heartache.

Know that this grief you feel, these tears that ebb and flow like the tide, and the lump in your throat that threatens to crush your spirit are temporary. Although they may never vanish completely, you *will* gain in strength and once again experience joy as the days, weeks, months, and years pass.

But take heart. I am with you in all these days. There is nothing that can separate Me from you—not even this grief, whether it's new or from days gone by.

No matter how deep your loss, My love and comfort for you goes deeper still. Just cling to Me. Know My arms are surrounding you, holding you up, rocking you to sleep. My tears join with yours, knowing that when this grief does pass, you will once again be doused in rivers of gladness. Until then, know that you are safe, loved, and comforted here in this place with Me.

I would have lost heart, unless I had believed that I would
see the goodness of the LORD in the land of the living.
PSALM 27:13 NKJV

The Highest Thoughts

*Guard Clear Thinking and Common Sense with your life; don't for a minute lose sight
of them. . . . You'll travel safely, you'll neither tire nor trip. You'll take afternoon naps
without a worry, you'll enjoy a good night's sleep. No need to panic over alarms or surprises,
or predictions. . .because GOD will be right there with you; he'll keep you safe and sound.*
PROVERBS 3:21, 23–26 MSG

Take on My mind-set. Come to Me for all your wisdom.

You are worried about so many things. Your thoughts are running away from you; your imaginings of what others are thinking—especially of you and your actions—are running amok. The stories your haphazard thoughts are telling you are making you anxious. Stop. Consider. Clear your mind.

Come into My presence, a place of safety and protection. Open My Word. Fill your mind with the wisdom of the ages. The maxims that have proved their worth. As you seek the light of My presence, allow Me to test your thoughts, to weigh your situation and circumstances clearly, to help you find the right path.

In doing so, you will find the peace that only My wisdom and thoughts can bring you. For you will be grounding yourself with the highest thoughts you could ever obtain—in heaven or on earth.

Uniquely Designed

If people can't see what God is doing, they stumble all over themselves;
but when they attend to what he reveals, they are most blessed.
PROVERBS 29:18 MSG

———◦◆◦———

Look at what I am doing in your life, where I am working.

You become stalled in your efforts when worries overtake you. More focused on your fears and foibles and less on your faith and fortes, your thoughts become scattered. You lose sight of the vision for your life. And where there is no vision, you become untethered, floating, drifting to an unknown destination, liable to blunder on the way.

In the past, I have given you a myriad of situations and challenges to learn from. I am working in your life in the present, strewing opportunities in your path, planting ideas and inspiration in your mind. I am moving out ahead, setting things up for your future.

Open your ears and hear My voice. Open your eyes and see what I am revealing. Open your mind and take in My Word. Let My thoughts become your thoughts. Attend to what I am telling you. For there is a plan being worked out for you, a purpose that you have been uniquely designed to fulfill. You and only you.

See this plan, this path, this purpose, and you will find the passion that drives you closer and closer to Me. In this you will find blessings galore.

Your path is prepared. See it. Walk it. Live it. And grow ever closer to Me in the process.

My Mind-set and Your Courage

"Don't worry about this Philistine," David told Saul. "I'll go fight him!" "Don't be ridiculous!" Saul replied. "There's no way you can fight this Philistine and possibly win! You're only a boy, and he's been a man of war since his youth." But David persisted.

1 SAMUEL 17:32–34 NLT

Hear My voice, and My voice alone, above all others, past and present. Persist in this endeavor.

The more time you spend with Me and in My Word, the more familiar with My thoughts you'll be. The more quickly they will come to your mind, drown out any other thoughts, especially those of discouragement.

See you as I see you—not as others do. For they do not know your heart. They do not know what I have gifted you with. Don't allow their words or their perception of you to blur your vision or to hinder My plan.

I have commanded you to be strong and courageous. To have My mind-set. To believe that I am with you—and that with My presence you will be able to do the impossible.

With the combination of My mind-set and your courage, you will find yourself winning battles against all odds—no matter what your human age, experience, knowledge, or education is. Such victories will not only benefit you but lead others to Me.

Master Planner

I said to the Lord, "You are my Master!
Every good thing I have comes from you."
PSALM 16:2 NLT

Forgo the need to control. I have a divine plan for you, one that requires you to relinquish all to Me. Trust that I have the best in mind for you.

Surrender your thoughts, dreams, ideas, ways, and mind-set to Me. What sweet release doing so gives you. No longer are you responsible for everything and everyone. That arduous burden can now be dropped.

Now pick up confidence in Me. Love for Me. Submission to Me. Allow Me to be Master of all that you are, have, and see. I know exactly what is going to happen and when. So wait on Me. Refuse to make things happen. Do not force your own or anyone else's hand. Don't force or kick doors open. Know that I have the timing of all things under control. Rest in this. Find peace in this.

As you continue on in this way, letting go of control, you will learn not only patience but perseverance, traits that will serve you well as you grow closer and closer to Me and walk further and further along your path.

Begin today. Take a deep breath and say, "Lord, I am letting go of my life, my heart, my future. I put all things in Your hands, trusting that You have a divine plan for me." Then rise, ready to be a tool in your Master's hands.

Nevertheless

And the king and his men went to Jerusalem against the Jebusites, the inhabitants of the land, who said to David, You shall not enter here, for the blind and the lame will prevent you; they thought, David cannot come in here. Nevertheless, David took the stronghold of Zion, that is, the City of David.
2 Samuel 5:6–7 ampc

There are no borders you cannot cross, no feat you cannot perform when you have faith in and are grounded in Me. What power lies in so firm a foundation! The remarks of naysayers—those who mean well and those you come up against—will have little effect. Indeed, they will only serve to spur you on, increase your energy and commitment to reaching the vision for your life.

No matter what others breathe into your life, no matter what thoughts they think toward you—spoken or unspoken—do not turn from your purpose, your mission in life. No matter what actions they take against you, do not be deterred. Instead, respond with a *nevertheless*. And, in My power, you will find yourself taking over strongholds others thought unconquerable.

Be alert, as well, for any internal voices of discouragement. When they come to mind as thoughts you can't seem to shake, replace those negative thoughts with promises found in My Word, prefacing them with *nevertheless*! And nothing will stand in the way of your victory!

Prepared for Victory

*"The LORD who rescued me from the claws of the lion
and the bear will rescue me from this Philistine!"*
1 SAMUEL 17:37 NLT

———◦◆◦———

I have been there for you in the past. This is a sign for you, proof to you, that I will be with you in the future. So do not agonize over where you are today. Remember that what you have been through before—the battles you have already won, the lessons you have already learned—has prepared you for what you will encounter today.

Without Me, you can do nothing. When you are tied to Me, intimately connected with Me, you have My life sap flowing through you. You have My strength, My courage, My energy, My power. There is nothing that we cannot accomplish together. Feel this. Live this.

Remain in Me at all costs. Listen to My voice. Follow My promptings. Obey My nudges. Spend time in My Word. Plant it deep within. Then when you are challenged, you will be able to stand up against whatever comes your way.

When you live such a life, what fruit you will bear! What foes you will topple! What victories you will win!

This is the plan the Father had from the beginning. This tie, this relationship, this closeness between the Creator and the created. Cherish it. And prepare for victory!

Lord of Breakthroughs

*And David came to Baal-perazim. . .and said, The Lord has broken
through my enemies before me, like the bursting out of great waters.
So he called the name of that place Baal-perazim [Lord of breaking through].*
2 SAMUEL 5:20 AMPC

No matter what your wall of challenge, I can help you break through to the other side. In fact, I clear the way for you—and have been doing so ever since you became a believer, ever since you started acting in and relying on your faith in Me. I have been, am, and will always be your Lord of breakthroughs!

Do not be discouraged; do not lose heart if things get tougher before the breaking through. Just continue to trust in Me, pray to Me, look to Me, knowing that when I move in your life, nothing can stand against Me.

Take up your courage. Take up your weapons of persistent prayer and faith. Persevere, knowing that the best is yet to come. Only believe! There IS a breakthrough ahead for you. You will overcome—as did David, over and over again. David who wrote:

....

....

....

....

....

....

....

....

....

....

*This I know, for God is for me. In God, Whose word I praise, in the Lord, Whose word I praise,
in God have I put my trust and confident reliance; I will not be afraid. What can man do to me?*
PSALM 56:9–11 AMPC

Surprised by Grief, Renewed by Joy

"Look! God's dwelling place is now among the people, and he will dwell with them.
They will be his people, and God himself will be with them and be their God.
'He will wipe every tear from their eyes. There will be no more death' or
mourning or crying or pain, for the old order of things has passed away."
REVELATION 21:3–4 NIV

A certain scent, an image, the sound of a seemingly familiar voice, and you find yourself caught up in the echoes, the memories of a loved one that you've lost. The grief takes you by surprise, overwhelming you. The unexpectedness of it catches you off guard, leaving you shaken and anxious.

Come to Me in these moments. Let Me hold you in My arms, shelter you until you can once again stand on solid ground. Allow Me to be the rock in your life.

How sweet are your memories of those who have already found their way to Father God. The light of their love will forever shine in your heart, warming your soul.

Yet know that a place has already been prepared for all who believe. Allow that to bring you comfort. And understand that while you should take time to cry, to mourn, to remember your loved ones, your inner strength and renewal lie in your joy of Father God.

Who You Truly Are

Saul gave David his own armor—a bronze helmet and a coat of mail. David put it on, strapped the sword over it, and took a step or two to see what it was like, for he had never worn such things before. "I can't go in these," he protested to Saul. "I'm not used to them." So David took them off again.

1 SAMUEL 17:38–39 NLT

Part of your anxiety comes from trying to walk in shoes that haven't been made for you, or putting on clothing that doesn't quite fit. By taking on things that don't suit, you find yourself tripping up, stumbling around.

Come to Me. Learn from Me. See what I have prepared for you. You have been made just for this time, this moment, this generation of humankind. You have a specific purpose to fulfill. Do it in your own way, the way that feels natural to you, and you will have more ease, more peace of mind. You will make more progress.

Simply stay attuned to Me for direction. Seek Me for wisdom. Gird yourself with Me for protection. Stand on Me for a solid foundation. For the closer you are to Me, the more you will become who you truly are—My handiwork. And the more you become who you truly are, the further into My kingdom you will be and the more it will grow.

When worries arise, look to see where you are wearing someone else's clothes. Then change things up. Put on the attire I created just for you.

Walk with Me

Then the two from Emmaus told their story of how Jesus
had appeared to them as they were walking along the road,
and how they had recognized him as he was breaking the bread.
LUKE 24:35 NLT

———◦•◦———

Come. Walk with Me. Spend time with Me in the outdoors, among My creation. Here you will learn much of Me. Here we can walk together in companionable silence or you can converse with Me, as did the two disciples who were walking to Emmaus.

As we walk, tell Me everything that is happening in your life, what is happening in your world. Tell Me all about how you feel, what you've seen. Then listen for My voice. Let Me teach you what you need to know. Learn from what I say. Take this new knowledge to heart.

Look for Me upon the path, within the breeze, up in the sky. Hear Me in the rustle of leaves, the song of a bird, the creak of a branch. In all these ways, I reveal Myself to you. I will open your eyes to things you have not known or did not understand before.

Recognize Me in all you see, touch, feel, hear, smell, and taste. Worship Me in all the beauty of nature that surrounds you. For I am in the day and the dark. I am in the snow and the rain. I am in the sun and the clouds. I am in all things. Walk with Me.

Find Your Way to Port

All praise to God, the Father of our Lord Jesus Christ, who has blessed us with every spiritual blessing in the heavenly realms because we are united with Christ. . . . Now he is far above any ruler or authority or power or leader or anything else—not only in this world but also in the world to come.

EPHESIANS 1:3, 21 NLT

I long to teach you of so many things. But to do so, you must surrender to Me. Know Me as the final authority. Recognize that in all things—temporal and spiritual—I reign.

Do not let events in your life dishearten or discourage you. Every morning, wake up to see things from My perspective. Instead of focusing on yourself and your fears, focus on Me in whom you have riches galore! An inexhaustible supply.

In the midst of your storm-tossed waters, as you realize you cannot handle things on your own, invite Me into your ark. Let Me take your ship's wheel. When I do, you will immediately feel an overwhelming peace of heart and mind. With Me traveling with you, you will find your way to port.

Unite with Me, and you will find yourself sailing in waters you never before imagined or expected you'd be able to navigate your way through. All to the praise and glory of Father God.

Waters of Faith

So [as the result of the Messiah's intervention] they shall [reverently] fear the name of the Lord from the west, and His glory from the rising of the sun. When the enemy shall come in like a flood, the Spirit of the Lord will lift up a standard against him and put him to flight [for He will come like a rushing stream which the breath of the Lord drives].

ISAIAH 59:19 AMPC

I am watching, seeing you go about your daily tasks. Worries crowd around the edges of your mind. Fear begins to trickle in. And before you know it, flooded waters are coursing through your brain, cutting a channel of panic so deep, you struggle to catch your breath.

This is the time to quickly seek Me. Build up another stream, a waterway of faith. Pray to Me. Imagine Me standing or sitting beside you, whispering words of faith and wisdom in your ear. Truly I am there with you. Begin praising Me, remembering all the love I have for you, all the ways I watch over you when you sleep and when you are awake, all the sacrifices I have made for you. I am the Light and Life that brings you joy, gives your life meaning. I am the one who has reconciled you with your Abba God.

Soon, the flooding waters of your faith will overrun your river of fear. Worries will dissipate as the current of truth grows deeper.

In the midst of your task, in the midst of your day, pause. Pray. Praise. Doing so will not only keep the torrent of fear at bay but dry up the streambed of worry.

Mind Transformation

Don't copy the behavior and customs of this world, but let God transform
you into a new person by changing the way you think. Then you will learn
to know God's will for you, which is good and pleasing and perfect.
ROMANS 12:2 NLT

What of your thoughts? Which are godly ones that will encourage you and others? What thoughts are those that build up instead of tear down? What thoughts are of service to you and which are of disservice?

Clear the clutter of your mind. Uproot all that the world's ways, customs, attitudes have planted within. Then take the seeds of My wisdom, My Word, and embed them deep in the soil of your mind.

In this way you will transform your mind from a decaying shadowland where nothing can grow to a flourishing garden of light, abundant in various fruits. Your mind will be totally renewed. This will make it easier for you to determine what I would have you do. And you will have an entirely new attitude, one that is reflected to others in the way you think, act, and shine for Me. Do this mind transformation as often as needed. It's a minute-to-minute formula for a beautiful and godly garden adorned with My pathway, My will for you.

Be assured that I have nothing but good planned for you, an outcome that will please you, Me, and our Father God. Trust Me in this. Test Me in this.

God Makes It Grow

*I planted, Apollos watered, but God [all the while] was making it grow
and [He] gave the increase. So neither he who plants is anything nor
he who waters, but [only] God Who makes it grow and become greater.*

1 CORINTHIANS 3:6–7 AMPC

You have heard My call. I have given you a purpose, a talent, a passion, one that will serve My kingdom and its people. Treasure that gift I have given you. Improve upon it. As you unite yourself with Me, pursue that purpose, talent, passion that I have placed in your heart. Endeavor to bless people with it. And leave the outcome up to Me. I will reward you in full in heaven and on earth. Simply continue to follow My plan for your life. I will take care of all the rest.

In this way, you will find yourself becoming less of a people pleaser and more of a God gratifier, for when you leave all in My hands, you will be less concerned over the results of your efforts. You will be doing all things for My smile, My congratulations, My admiration—not for the approval, applause, and pat on the back of a fellow human being.

What freedom this will allow you as you continue to grow in Me and as I endeavor to make what you do grow and become greater!

You Have the Power

*Aramean raiders had invaded the land of Israel, and among their captives was a young
girl who had been given to Naaman's wife as a maid. One day the girl said to her mistress,
"I wish my master would go to see the prophet in Samaria. He would heal him of his leprosy."*

2 Kings 5:2–3 NLT

No matter how low the world may view your station, when you are obedient to Me, you have power. For you are living a holy life.

A young shepherd boy felled a giant with a mere slingshot and a stone. A captive servant girl prompted a military leader, a leprous heathen, to visit a man of God and be healed. Afterward, the commander became a worshipper of Father God. Even a herder's wife became a national heroine for smiting an enemy army commander.

Refuse to let your status, your position, or your perceptions of yourself and your life keep you from working for Me. Use the resources I have placed at your fingertips. Know that you have the power to do all that I desire you to do. For I am within you, leading you, helping you. So speak the words I would have you say. Do the things I ask you to do. And never doubt that you have all the strength you need in Me to change the world and people around you. I have planted you just where I need you to be.

Beyond Expectations

*But Naaman became angry and stalked away. "I thought he would
certainly come out to meet me!" he said. "I expected him to wave his hand
over the leprosy and call on the name of the LORD his God and heal me!"*
2 KINGS 5:11 NLT

I have answered your prayer and am now doing something that you didn't expect. You had in mind a completely different plan, way of working, response from Me. Instead of stalking away, follow the plan I have laid out before you. Have no fear that it's exactly the way I want it to go. In fact, this is the best outcome for you—and one you could never have imagined!

Throw out your preconceived ideas of what should happen. Just go and do what I am calling you to, leading you to. Just be obedient to what I tell you rather than doing nothing, sulking, or panicking.

Know that at times your expectations and My movements in your world, My response to your prayers, may be totally different things. Yet be assured that My way, although it may be humbling privately and publicly or may seem to be an impossible path, is the better way.

....

....

....

....

....

....

....

....

....

....

*"My thoughts are nothing like your thoughts," says the LORD.
"And my ways are far beyond anything you could imagine."*
ISAIAH 55:8 NLT

Changing Mantles

Yet amid all these things we are more than conquerors and
gain a surpassing victory through Him Who loved us.
ROMANS 8:37 AMPC

Sometime in your life you may have trials, suffer illness, lose a loved one, go hungry, become homeless, be bullied or threatened. But in all these situations, you are not a victim. For you are My follower. You are more than a conqueror. You are and will always be victorious.

So do not cower in a corner. Do not worry or become anxious over what may happen tomorrow. Do not take on the woe-is-me mantle. Instead, rise up and stand. Break the worry chain; step away from what has happened, is happening, or will happen. See yourself as the conqueror over all your circumstances—public and personal, spiritual and physical. Step away from the self-pity and pour yourself into serving others. Reach out to help others, even those who are suffering the same circumstances you are. Share the never-ending and unconditional love I've lavished on you with others in your path.

I will lead you out of the darkness of victimhood and into the light of victory. From the mantle of helpless to the helper. This will be your salvation and your unexpected joy. This will be your way out of the all-about-me abyss and draw you ever closer to the all-about-Me apex.

Restored by Faith

For she kept saying to herself, If I only touch
His garment, I shall be restored to health.
MATTHEW 9:21 AMPC

———◦•◦———

Seek Me. Reach out for Me. Look to touch Me. Be intent in this seeking, reaching, looking. Have it in the forefront of your mind, the cornerstone of your faith. Remind yourself, continually, constantly, that if you but extend yourself in My direction, feel as if you have actually touched Me, spirit to Spirit, I will restore you. I will make you whole.

Such a seeking and reaching takes courage; it takes confidence in Me that what you are requesting will not be denied. And that courage and confidence you have. For I feel you, even now. And in that feeling, that tugging of your spirit upon Mine, I am turning to you. I see you, everything there is to know about you—past, present, and future. I see your thoughts, dreams, wishes, desires. I understand what you are striving for and why. And as I am loving you through all your seeking and reaching, you are now more wholly Mine.

You have taken a risk, and My response is your reward. Take courage. Your faith has and always will restore you.

_____

_____

_____

_____

_____

_____

_____

_____

_____

_____

Jesus turned around and, seeing her, He said, Take courage, daughter!
Your faith has made you well. And at once the woman was restored to health.
MATTHEW 9:22 AMPC

Message from the Mount

"In a word, what I'm saying is, Grow up. You're kingdom subjects.
Now live like it. Live out your God-created identity. Live generously
and graciously toward others, the way God lives toward you."
MATTHEW 5:48 MSG

⌐◦◆◦⌐

You are looking for joy, for direction, for blessings. I have given you all that you need for your life if you would but follow the pattern I have drafted for you, the one I have spoken on the mount. There I tell you how to treat other people. How to not be angry but forgive. How to give your coat if someone takes your shirt. To love those who disparage and disrespect you.

On the mount, I tell you how to do good things in secret. For then Father God will reward you openly. I teach you how to pray, what to say. I even instruct you in what to save and give away, whom to serve, what to seek. And I tell you how to avoid wasting your time and energy worrying about everything—big and little. How to find the narrow way and obey.

Live My message from the mount. Build your life upon it.

....

....

....

....

....

....

....

....

....

....

....

"These words I speak to you are not incidental additions to your life,
homeowner improvements to your standard of living. They are
foundational words, words to build a life on."
MATTHEW 7:24 MSG

Your Covering

O God the Lord, the Strength of my salvation, You have covered my head in the day
of battle. . . . I know and rest in confidence upon it that the Lord will maintain the cause
of the afflicted, and will secure justice for the poor and needy [of His believing children].
PSALM 140:7, 12 AMPC

See Me as a soft blanket wrapped around you, protecting, comforting, warming. Sheltering you from wind and rain. Make Me your home, your primary residence, the roof over your head, shielding you from the elements of nature, all the quandaries and pitfalls of life. Immerse yourself within Me until you cannot tell where you begin and I end.

Enveloping you day and night, I will give you all the peace you need to cope with anything that may come your way. Underneath My covering, you will fall asleep quickly and easily, knowing that your protection is sure. When you awake, you will be refreshed, confident, ready to face the day, finding opportunities instead of challenges, joy instead of anxiety.

Make *Me* your security blanket, your covering. Rely on Me—not yourself or other beings, the world at large. Clutch at Me, use Me, raise Me, hide beneath Me, take Me wherever you go. Make Me an indispensable part of your very existence—now, here, forevermore.

God Pours

We know how troubles can develop passionate patience in us, and how that patience in turn forges the tempered steel of virtue, keeping us alert for whatever God will do next. In alert expectancy such as this, we're never left feeling shortchanged. Quite the contrary—we can't round up enough containers to hold everything God generously pours into our lives through the Holy Spirit!
ROMANS 5:3–5 MSG

Such sweet music we make together as we abide, breathe, converse in the rhythm that is so uniquely ours to share, ours to partake in, ours to satisfy.

In those times when you come to speak to Me, you may discover some interference. Do not be dismayed. Do not forgo seeking Me. Instead, persevere. Refocus on Me. Remember the times of abiding we have shared before. Seek that same experience. Relax. Enjoy the stillness. Patiently wait for My abiding presence coming softly on the air and with the pace of your every breath.

Listen for words, for wisdom. But most of all, just be. I will make clear all that you need to know. I will give you the peace unbreakable. I will pour Myself into you so that you will rise with the strength of having been in and experienced the Light that first called you, abides within you, surrounds you, and guides you.

Abiding in Me, you will not misstep, for I am the Way. I am your path. With this knowledge, go forward boldly, with courage and joy.

As Promised

*Nevertheless, My loving-kindness will I not break off from him, nor allow
My faithfulness to fail [to lie and be false to him]. My covenant will I
not break or profane, nor alter the thing that is gone out of My lips.*
PSALM 89:33–34 AMPC

Humankind promises you a myriad of things. But only My promises stand the test of time. Only My assurances are infallible. Only My words will lead you and keep you on the right road, the road to My abiding presence, My kingdom, My love.

If you are weary, take smaller steps. Lean into Me. My arms will catch you, hold you, envelop you. I will help you, carry you, if I must. I will get you where you need, want, desire to be. There is no hurry. No rush. I have power over time and can and will skew things your way.

So do not worry. I am watching, waiting, walking. Resting with you by the side of the road, binding your wounds, putting oil upon your cuts, soothing all your hurts until you are better, more whole, ready to rise up again and stand in Me.

You are in My favor as no other. You are the apple of My eye. Remember this. Allow it to give you the confidence, comfort, and courage to continue in your walk with Me, at My pace, in line with My plan, as promised.

Father of Light

So, my very dear friends, don't get thrown off course. Every desirable and beneficial gift comes out of heaven. The gifts are rivers of light cascading down from the Father of Light. There is nothing deceitful in God, nothing two-faced, nothing fickle. He brought us to life using the true Word, showing us off as the crown of all his creatures.

JAMES 1:16–18 MSG

Do not despair if your routine is disrupted. Instead, know that I am with you, as always.

Make abiding in My presence the only routine you actually have. Make My presence, My nearness, My breath upon your face your only constant.

My Word has told you that I never change. I cannot be moved. Make these truths your rock, your firm foundation. For then you will not be shaken by anything that comes your way.

Keep Me as your focal point, an immovable place for you to rest your eyes while everything else may be spinning around you. A place for you to set your heart while all other longings have grown distant. See Me as your North Star, the brightest point in your life, the one thing you can always see and find. The star that tells you where you are and points you home. To Me; your resting place. The reassurance for any traveler on a long journey in the sea of life.

Joy of the Lord

"Go home and prepare a feast. . .and share it with those who don't have anything:
This day is holy to God. Don't feel bad. The joy of GOD is your strength!" . . . So the
people went off to feast, eating and drinking and including the poor in a great celebration.
Now they got it; they understood the reading that had been given to them.

NEHEMIAH 8:10, 12 MSG

Allow My Word to convict you but not depress you. To humble you but not humiliate you. To give you hope, not make you anxious. The Word is to build you up, prepare you, direct you, give you the strength that you need to live the life I have planned for you. It is more a home I have built for you than it is a blueprint to follow.

Understand this. Know that I want you to be touched, to have a tender heart, but I do not want to break you. I want to bind you, love you, heal you, reach you, teach you.

So if you have, share with those who have not. Experience the joy that it brings you, how it lifts you out of yourself, draws you closer to Me. Understand the Word I have put at your fingertips. Get its message. Then celebrate the life that you have undertaken in following Me. Realize the joy that is available to you in every moment because you walk with Me. May the joy you find in Me be all the strength you need.

The True Road

*"Cursed are those who put their trust in mere humans, who rely
on human strength and turn their hearts away from the LORD.
They are like stunted shrubs in the desert, with no hope for the future."*
JEREMIAH 17:5–6 NLT

Examine your life, your priorities, where you're spending your time.

The worry over finances, the pursuit of money and possessions, sometimes becomes not only a distraction but a dangerous preoccupation to My followers. For then their sight is blocked, their vision skewed. Their time for Me becomes not just limited but nonexistent.

Their worldly goods can become altars at which they sacrifice all their time, freedom, and focus. Soon, worshipping things instead of Me, they drift away from a true relationship with Me. They rely more on their own efforts and strength than on Me.

The road to Me—the true road to prosperity, the one you are to embark on and keep your feet upon—is one on which you are to put all your hope, trust, confidence. Then you will find the deeper meanings, the greater wisdom, the truer life, one in which you'll bear fruit—in this world and the next.

*"But blessed are those who trust in the LORD and have made the LORD their hope
and confidence. They are like trees planted along a riverbank. . . . Such trees
are not bothered by the heat or worried by long months of drought."*
JEREMIAH 17:7–8 NLT

The Spirit of Your Father

Do not be anxious about how or what you are to speak; for what you are to say will be given you in that very hour and moment, for it is not you who are speaking, but the Spirit of your Father speaking through you. . . . What I say to you in the dark, tell in the light; and what you hear whispered in the ear, proclaim upon the housetops.
MATTHEW 10:19–20, 27 AMPC

I am constantly speaking to you with My presence, My Word, My followers, My movement in your situations. Be reassured with this knowledge. Attune your spirit to Mine. Keep as close to Me as you can. Then you will not have to worry over anything, what you should do or what you should say. For I will be speaking into your life, all around you. The Spirit of Father God will tell you exactly what you need to say, exactly what He wants you to say, exactly what needs to be said. Or He will ask you to remain silent if that is what is called for.

So simply continue to stay close to Me. I will tell you amazing things that you will then, as the Spirit moves you, reveal to all those whose worlds connect to your own. Just keep your eyes and ears open as you live in the comfort and peace this knowledge gives you.

Going All the Way

"If you don't go all the way with me, through thick and thin, you don't deserve me.
If your first concern is to look after yourself, you'll never find yourself. But if
you forget about yourself and look to me, you'll find both yourself and me."
MATTHEW 10:38–39 MSG

Choose this day, this moment, this lifetime whom you are going to serve, whom you are going to walk with through all the highs and lows of your life.

A walk with Me cannot be halfhearted. You need to be in the whole way. Haven't I given you the greatest commandment? To love Me with *all* your heart, *all* your soul, and *all* your mind. Not half, or a quarter, or three-quarters—but *all* of you. Your entire being.

Do not flee from Me at the first sign of trouble. For if you do, you'll never find what amazing things would've happened if you'd stuck it out with Me. It's like being around for My arrest and crucifixion but missing out on My resurrection and the gift of the Holy Spirit.

So forget about your own perspective on the world, its ways, and your part in it. Stop perceiving things with the eyes of your ego. Start seeing things from My perspective. Seek My presence. Live in My world and its kingdom ways. In doing so, you'll find yourself living the life of a princess instead of a pauper. Choose this day to go *all* the way with Me.

Come Away

*"Come to me. Get away with me and you'll recover your life. I'll show you
how to take a real rest. Walk with me and work with me—watch how I do it.
Learn the unforced rhythms of grace. I won't lay anything heavy or ill-fitting
on you. Keep company with me and you'll learn to live freely and lightly."*
MATTHEW 11:28–30 MSG

There is no sweeter rest than the rest you find in My presence, My arms. For that rest is a supernatural repose in the One who created every part of your being. Not just your body, but your soul and your spirit. I know every bit of you. I know exactly what you need and desire. For I am the One who designed you.

So put yourself and your burdens into My hands. Make it your mission in life to live in Me. I will neither misdirect or mishandle you. On the contrary, I will prepare you, teach you all you need to know. In Me, you will find all the refreshment, blessings, and quiet you need. I am your example of how to bear up under anything that comes your way—and I will give you the strength and the power, the means and the ways, to do just that. So come. Come away with Me. And find everything your true self has been looking for—and more—in this world, on the way to the next.

New Life

And He said to them, Come after Me [as disciples—letting Me be your Guide],
follow Me, and I will make you fishers of men! At once they left their nets
and became His disciples [sided with His party and followed Him].
MATTHEW 4:19–20 AMPC

I have called you to a new life, to a life rich in heavenly treasurers. And I continue to call you, day after day. Yet you at times hesitate. You do not immediately follow when I summon you.

Do not be anxious about what I call you to do. It is not something you would be ill fitted or unprepared for. The activity to which I call you is not only what I have already qualified you for, and prepared you for, but the thing in which I will give you success.

So do not let fear or worries stand between you and your new life. Instead, trust in Me. Abide in Me. Spend time with Me so that I can teach you and prepare you. Then when you are ready, I will ask you to leave that part of your life that is no longer serving the kingdom, to leave all that you were and all you were anticipating in that "old life," and to follow Me to something new.

Depend on Me. Trust Me. Have faith that once you are on that new path, you will never look back but be reaching further and further into the new life lived in the light and love of My presence.

You Must Choose

The Lord your God Who goes before you, He will fight for you just as He did for you in Egypt before your eyes, and in the wilderness, where you have seen how the Lord your God bore you, as a man carries his son, in all the way that you went until you came to this place.
DEUTERONOMY 1:30–31 AMPC

I am making a way for you through the wilderness of your life, forging a path, readying your way. I have already died for you, before you even knew who I was. And I continue to fight for you every step of the way. I will never give you up, never give you over to the enemy. I will carry you when you can no longer walk, guide you when you can no longer see, speak to you when you can no longer hear. I will hold you in My arms as a father would his child, a nursing woman her baby.

Yet I give you the freedom to walk away from all I can provide, all I can do for you. But what a waste of a life that would be, one in which you continue to wander and never get to the Promised Land.

Each day, you must choose how you will live: trusting in Me or going it alone. Be wise. Let Me carry you. Take Me as your forever companion. Allow Me to lead you to the land of milk and honey.

Faith Walk

*For we walk by faith [we regulate our lives and conduct ourselves by our
conviction or belief respecting man's relationship to God and divine things,
with trust and holy fervor; thus we walk] not by sight or appearance.*

2 CORINTHIANS 5:7 AMPC

When you are walking very close to Me, you obtain supernatural vision. When you are tuned in to Me, I will give you amazing insights and revelations as to what I am doing in your life, in your world. You will have the confidence of My prophets. The visions of Elijah, the courage of Deborah, the strength of Samson, the obedience of Mary. You will see avenues I have opened up before you, hear answers to questions you have yet to ask, and find angels protecting you at every turn. All because you have elected to walk by faith and not by sight.

So stay as close by My side, as near to My presence as you possibly can. Rely on Me for all things. Bring Me every concern, issue, challenge, loss. Allow Me to transform all these things into something that will not only serve you but build up the kingdom of heaven.

Trust Me as you never have before. Be bold in every area of your life. Remain humble in your accomplishments. And open your eyes to a world of God's glory.

On Your Side

"Don't be afraid!" Elisha told him. "For there are more on our side than on theirs!"
Then Elisha prayed, "O LORD, open his eyes and let him see!" The LORD opened
the young man's eyes, and when he looked up, he saw that the hillside
around Elisha was filled with horses and chariots of fire.
2 KINGS 6:16–17 NLT

When things come up against you, when it looks as if all is lost, remember that I am with you. I will never leave nor forsake you. And although you may not see exactly what I am doing, or cannot fathom the answer I have to your prayer, or have no idea how a situation will come out right, simply have faith that all will be well. Have faith that there are many more on your side than against—in this world and the next.

There is so much going on that you cannot see physically, so much more happening on so many levels, in this world and the next, that you must rely on Me—or give up believing in Me altogether. It is a choice you may make often in one day. To believe My promises or the world's lies. To live close to Me or give in to your old self. To walk with faith or cringe in fear. To live with hope or die in despair. To experience an otherworldly peace or earthly panic.

You choose. Choose Me. See Me and all the host on your side.

Befriending the Enemy

Learn from Me. Follow My example. When you are dealing with enemies, do not let fear of them or anxiety over their actions have the upper hand. Instead, give your fears and anxieties to Me. I will help you more than overcome both. I will calm you, give you the peace you need to stand up to any enemy.

And when, through My power, you have gained victory over your enemies, be gracious and generous to them. Bestow gifts upon them. Treat them so much better than they ever treated you. Befriend them. Then allow them their freedom to go back where they came from. Release their deeds against you from your mind and life. Forget the fears and angst they brought out in you.

Love your enemies, as I have commanded you. In doing so, you will experience the peace that comes with obeying Me. For I have found that the best way to lose an enemy is to make them your friend.

....

....

....

....

....

....

....

....

....

So the king made a great feast for them and then sent them home to their master. After that, the Aramean raiders stayed away from the land of Israel.

2 KINGS 6:23 NLT

Above Your World

And He raised us up together with Him and made us sit down together
[giving us joint seating with Him] in the heavenly sphere [by virtue
of our being] in Christ Jesus (the Messiah, the Anointed One).

EPHESIANS 2:6 AMPC

I can carry you above all the anxieties, angst, fears, frustrations, conflicts, calamities, dangers, and despair this world has to offer. Although I might not transport you as Father God did Elijah in a chariot, I will help you ascend above all the troubles in your life.

But you must willingly climb into the chariot with Me to attain such heights. That means walking close to Me. Abiding in Me, growing in Me, as the grape does on the vine. Allow Me to nurture and mature you. That means giving all of yourself to Me.

Do so now. Breathe deep. Lower your shoulders. Lean back against My chest. Listen for the sound of My own heart. Relax in My peace. Allow your thoughts the freedom to fade away. Remain this way until you feel that overwhelming sense of peace. Until in the silence of My presence you feel Me lifting you up, above all cares, and landing you in a place of peace where you can spend time resting in the green of the garden, above your world—the earth—and into Mine—the realms of heaven.

Inner Realms

"The heart is hopelessly dark and deceitful, a puzzle that no one can figure out.
But I, God, search the heart and examine the mind. I get to the heart of the human.
I get to the root of things. I treat them as they really are, not as they pretend to be."
JEREMIAH 17:9–10 MSG

You constantly strive to predict people, to read their minds and hearts, to see what they may or may not say or do. This frustrates and worries you, not knowing what may come from the words and actions of others.

Know that you will never figure out others. But I can and do. I can go deeper into the inner realms of all people. I can get down to the very mind and heart of the matter. So leave the intentions of others, as well as their words and actions, in My hands. Know that I see how they have treated you and will judge them accordingly, just as I see how you treat others then judge you.

All the judging is in My hands. Concern yourself only with looking to Me and knowing that I will be with you in all situations, in all meetings, in all areas of your life. I have it under control. Your job is merely to love others—no matter how they treat you. Do that, and you shall reap all the benefits and blessings of obedience to Me and My commands.

Doors

There is no fear in love; but perfect love casts out fear, because fear involves torment. But he who fears has not been made perfect in love.

1 JOHN 4:18 NKJV

Just when you think all doors are closed, I will open one. It will begin with a glimpse of light beneath the door, a light that beckons you, draws you closer. Once you attend to it, things will begin happening. You will get a note from a friend, read a scripture, hear a sermon. All will be signposts to help you find your way to the next venture.

Then it is up to you to come to Me, to speak to Me for further guidance. To confer with Me every step of the way up to the door and beyond. It is up to you to trust Me, to consult Me, to ask at every turn, "What do *You* think, Lord? Is this the way You would have me go?"

Then I would have you *trust* Me. For your doubts and fears will keep you from moving forward in the full power I am aching to give you. They may even make you stumble upon the path. Or perhaps cause you to miss your opportunity of even opening a door!

So put those worries behind you. Banish your fears. Seek all the guidance I am providing. And trust that I know the way you are to go, the way that will give you a life wholly lived and wonder filled.

Against All Hope

He believed—the God who gives life to the dead and calls into being things
that were not. Against all hope, Abraham in hope believed. . . being fully
persuaded that God had power to do what he had promised.
ROMANS 4:17–18, 21 NIV

That's what it all comes down to, your belief. How much you believe in Me, have faith in Me, is what will determine your walk with Me.

I give life to the dead. I make a way where there is no other way. I either help you escape or I walk with you through it. And actually being with you and you being in Me during your troubles and trials is, in itself, an escape, as it was for the three with whom I walked in a fiery furnace. They believed. Do you believe? Are you fully convinced—beyond all hope, beyond what your physical senses, family, and friends tell you—that I can do the impossible? That I have such power? Are you totally convinced?

If not, gird up your faith by prayer and petition to Me. Immerse yourself in My Word, soaking up every precious sentence and precept, down to the very letters themselves. Sit in My presence, saturating yourself with My essence. Know that through Me you can change yourself and your world for the better. That I can give you all hope when no one else can find hope.

Focus

Let us throw off everything that hinders and the sin that so
easily entangles. And let us run with perseverance the race marked
out for us, fixing our eyes on Jesus, the pioneer and perfecter of faith.
HEBREWS 12:1–2 NIV

My beloved, your eyes seem to be everywhere but on Me. But I would have you change your focus, do a check-in each moment of the day to see where your head has turned.

Let your eyes not be on your circumstances, the roaring wind and the pounding waves. Know that if you focus on Me, if you walk toward Me, you will not sink into the deep.

Let your eyes not be on your own plans and ideas, your own wants, needs, and expectations. You will not be fully empowered until you surrender all your interests and preconceived ideas to Me.

Let your eyes not be on your own welfare. Do not begin your walk with Me and then run when the going gets tough. Look to make sure your faith—not your fears—is what you are attending to, where you are putting your energies.

And lastly, let your eyes not be on others and what I may or may not be doing in their life compared to yours. This is not your purview but Mine and Mine alone.

Focus on Me alone. May your minute-by-minute mantra be "I keep my eyes always on the LORD. With him at my right hand, I will not be shaken" (Psalm 16:8 NIV).

Best Judge of All

"But as for you, you meant evil against me; but God meant it for good,
in order to bring it about as it is this day, to save many people alive."
GENESIS 50:20 NKJV

I know what's best for you, so do not let your circumstances or the words of others disturb you. Do not be so quick to judge your situations or how they affect you as bad or good. What you deem bad for you today may turn out to be good for you tomorrow. Nor should you judge the people you encounter as good or bad—no matter what they say, how they treat you, whose "side" they are on—whether they be friends, acquaintances, or rulers.

Follow My lead. Love all people. Fear no one. Accept all circumstances. Forgive and let go of all bitterness. Allow Me to be the judge for and in all things.

This is the purpose I have for you: to glorify Me by doing what I have called you to do, loving Me, and loving yourself and others. And if you truly love Me, you will trust Me with all things. You will take the seemingly good with the seemingly bad. In all states of mind and being, turn to Me for the truth and the way. Let Me be the judge. Remain joyful and trusting in all situations. And I will work out all things for your good.

Raise Your Hands

I desire therefore that the men pray everywhere,
lifting up holy hands, without wrath and doubting.
1 Timothy 2:8 NKJV

The most powerful weapon at your disposal is you coming to Me in prayer. Come into My presence wherever you are! Speak to Me. Bring Me all your requests, absolutely everything that is on your mind. Leave all your worries at My feet. Thank Me for all I have already done and am still doing—with every breath you take—in your life. Lift your eyes to Me in gratitude and in love. And My peace will overwhelm you, take you to new heights, fill you with a supernatural joy.

When you come to Me in prayer, raise your hands. Doing so will remind you that *I* am the ultimate authority. That I am the one with the power to change your situation. That will make it easier for you to set your challenges aside and focus once again on Me. And when you raise up those hands, let go of whatever anger and conflicts, doubts and what-ifs that are polluting your life and preying on your mind and spirit. Know that I will give you all the wisdom you need.

Release all to Me. You doing so will give Me the freedom to transform you and your life and to give you that precious knowledge and the peace that defies human understanding.

PRAY

*"The Son of Man, on the other hand, feasts and drinks, and you say,
'He's a glutton and a drunkard, and a friend of tax collectors and
other sinners!' But wisdom is shown to be right by its results."*
MATTHEW 11:19 NLT

When you feel disconnected from Me, when worries begin to take over your mind-set, examine your prayer life. It is to be a constant, consistent, continual exercise, not a once-in-a-while exercise. Every moment of the day:

P   Pursue My presence.

R   Reach out to Me with all your heart, mind, body, and strength.

A   Ask and you'll receive, seek and you'll find, knock and I will open.

Y   Yield to My wisdom and strength.

As you are continually praying, I am continually standing at the door, knocking. And when you hear Me call, when you open the door, I come in and commune with you, telling you all you need to know.

It is then that you must yield to My wisdom. You must do as I bid, regardless of how it may sound to you and others. Do not let their opinions or your own inner thoughts deter you from the plan I have laid out for you, the purpose for which I have created you. Someday you will see the wisdom of the things I tell you to say and do. For now, have faith that I am guiding you exactly where you are to be walking for Father God's glory. Trust Me in this.

The Little Things

"If you are faithful in little things,
you will be faithful in large ones."
LUKE 16:10 NLT

At times you may be in My presence day after day, but no word seems to be coming. Have no fear. Do not worry that I am not speaking, looking, watching, or responding. Instead, keep your eyes open for the little things you are missing. Pay attention to the Word that comes your way, whether it's revealed in circumstances, the voices of others, or the things you read. Take note of them. Record them. Perceive them as stepping-stones on the path you are following. Plant them in the fertile soil of your mind, allowing them to grow there, to feed and nourish you, to prepare you for the steps ahead. If you feel My prompting, perhaps even share them with others.

If you are faithful in seeking and following all the teachings I provide, if you diligently apply them to your life and heart, I will entrust you with more and more.

Remember that I am not just Lord of the big important moments and decisions, but I am also Lord of the small things, the little choices you make each and every day. Allow Me to be Master of your entire life, and nothing will be hidden from you.

"Do not despise these small beginnings, for the LORD rejoices
to see the work begin, to see the plumb line in Zerubbabel's hand."
ZECHARIAH 4:10 NLT

Provision

This is what the Lord has commanded: Let every man gather of it as much as
he will need, an omer for each person, according to the number of your persons;
take it. . . . When they measured it with an omer, he who gathered much had nothing
over, and he who gathered little had no lack; each gathered according to his need.
EXODUS 16:16, 18 AMPC

So many times I have moved to rescue you, extended My arms to ensure your footing upon your path, or held provisions in My hand, waiting for you to look My way then take what you needed. Yet sometimes you didn't even look My way, so busy or distracted by your worries, fears, doubts, ideas of what should happen, or strivings to resolve things in your own way and under your own power. It's as if you are walking in the wilderness, crying for food, doubting that I will even provide.

Let this not be so! Learn from the Word—the examples, the stories, the situations of ones who walked in the wilderness before you. Know that I will provide you with water and manna, spiritually, by My presence. And that I will also provide you with physical sustenance.

Your job is to trust. To ask. To look for and then take what I have provided in accordance with what you need—no more, no less, ensuring there will be enough for all. Trust Me in this.

From Sighing to Gladness

But I called on your name, LORD, from deep within the pit. You heard
me when I cried, "Listen to my pleading! Hear my cry for help!"
LAMENTATIONS 3:55–56 NLT

———◦◦◦———

You come before Me with such a heavy sigh. In that exhale, you release all your efforts, self-reliance, doubts, fears, and worries. You let them drift out of your world and into Mine, where they dissipate at the foot of My cross. Feel this movement from load to lightness. For you have emptied yourself. You are now freed up, open, available, able to receive all that I have been holding here for you. An otherworldly, supernatural calm and assurance and peace, a sense of contentment, an inner knowing that all is truly well envelops you. The more this knowing deepens down to your very core, the more you feel My presence growing in your life. And the more of Me you experience in all aspects of your life, the more joyful you become, like a child, happy just to sit in her mother's lap, knowing that there no harm can come to her. All is safe and well.

_____

_____

_____

_____

_____

_____

_____

_____

_____

_____

And the ransomed of the Lord shall return and come to Zion with
singing, and everlasting joy shall be upon their heads; they shall
obtain joy and gladness, and sorrow and sighing shall flee away.
ISAIAH 35:10 AMPC

Blessed, Broken, and Multiplied

Jesus took the five loaves and two fish, looked up toward heaven, and blessed them. Then, breaking the loaves into pieces, he gave the bread to the disciples, who distributed it to the people. They all ate as much as they wanted, and afterward, the disciples picked up twelve baskets of leftovers.

MATTHEW 14:19–20 NLT

I have such compassion for you. There is nothing—no misdeed, injury, provocation, or insult against you—that does not wound Me as well. I long to heal, to sustain.

Know that whatever provisions you bring to Me, I will bless and break them. When I return what little you have, you will have more than enough for not only yourself but others who are yearning to hear, learn of, and feel Me.

This power I have to bless, break, and multiply was proven on a hilltop thousands of years ago. The event was so memorable that My followers still read and talk about it today. Does this not remove any doubts in your mind about My power, My love, My eagerness to provide for you? Know that My compassion reaches through the ages, extends to all those who although they have never met Me in My earthly form still believe in Me. Amazing power. Amazing strength.

Bring Me what you have. And let Me prove My love for you over and over again.

At His Feet

And a great multitude came to Him, bringing with them the lame, the maimed,
the blind, the dumb, and many others, and they put them down at His feet.
MATTHEW 15:30 AMPC

I am here to offer you ease. To give you relief from all your burdens, all your cares and woes.

With all your strength, take up those whom you love, those who worry your mind, those whose future is uncertain physically, mentally, emotionally, spiritually. Grasp them tightly; hug them to your chest. And then travel to Me, step by staggering step. Recognize that this is a load you cannot carry. This weight of others' maladies, no matter how much you love them, is not to be borne by you. In silence, bring them before Me.

I see the sorrow, the helplessness in your eyes, the longing to do more. Yet knowing that, for your part, there is no more that can be done. In silence, surrender each loved one to Me. Lay them at My feet one by one. Submit them to Me, for Me to do as I will, as God has planned and provided for each soul and spirit that walks the earth.

There is no need to speak. I can see your heartache and their calamity. I absorb it all, transform it all.

Then rise, feel the ease and relief your giving up of them to Me has provided. And realize the wonder of it all.

Returning Home

Then when he came to himself, he said, How many hired servants of my father have enough food, and [even food] to spare, but I am perishing (dying) here of hunger!
LUKE 15:17 AMPC

Some days you may feel as if you are a long way off. You realize that you have been feeding yourself on worries and frustrations, fears and dreads. You are starved for the truth of the Word, its encouragements, its cleansing power. A sense of hopelessness and unworthiness has stayed your movements, your reaching toward Me. You are aching for Me yet are ashamed for feeling such a lack of connection. So you hesitate to return, to seek Me.

Know and be confident of this: I am always waiting outside the door for you to come home to Me. I am looking down the path to see if you are there, perhaps just around the corner from where I stand.

So come to yourself, your divine senses, then come to Me. My arms are open wide, ready to embrace you, to celebrate your homecoming and feast again on our mutual love. Return to where you belong—within My truth and My Word. Welcome home!

While he was still a long way off, his father saw him and was moved with pity and tenderness [for him]; and he ran and embraced him and kissed him [fervently].
LUKE 15:20 AMPC

Preparation

For we are God's [own] handiwork (His workmanship), recreated in Christ Jesus,
[born anew] that we may do those good works which God predestined (planned
beforehand) for us [taking paths which He prepared ahead of time], that we should walk
in them [living the good life which He prearranged and made ready for us to live].
EPHESIANS 2:10 AMPC

Do not strive for perfection or force goodness. Simply follow in My footsteps. As you continually connect with Me, all will fall into place. You will naturally establish the rhythm that powers My kingdom. All stress and worry will pass away because you are focused on Me. You will know the right words to say, the right things to do.

Even then if seemingly mistakes are made, they will be of no concern for you because they are part of the divine plan, the teaching you need to move into the next phase, to take the next step. This is part of your preparation for doing the good works I have assigned to your hand, the things you were created to do, say, perform. Learn your lessons, store their value within, and then move on in My presence and power.

So ease up on yourself, your life. Be gentle, knowing that perfection is nothing you can strive for. That it is only I who make you perfect. Without Me, you are incomplete. With Me, you are God's masterpiece.

Know all things are in My hand. And because you are connected with Me, all is well.

Amazing Transformations

You were taught, with regard to your former way of life, to put off your old self,
which is being corrupted by its deceitful desires; to be made new in the attitude of your
minds; and to put on the new self, created to be like God in true righteousness and holiness.
EPHESIANS 4:22–24 NIV

You are so focused on the things your mind says you cannot do that you are missing out on My saving power, My overcoming, My strength, My victories, the ones I have lined up for you.

Come into My presence. Empty your mind of all the "I can't," "I should," "I won't be able to" statements that are filling the space reserved for My promises, My urgings, My will and purpose for your life. Release them one by one, letting them drift away toward My light that has the power to defuse them. Then refill your mind with My Word. At all times keep those statements, those truths with which I have inspired your spirit, before you. Plant them in your heart. As you do so, an amazing transformation will begin to take place in you. You will become more and more like Me. More able to do what you and others believed could not be done.

The more you rely on this remedy of My presence and My Word, the more you will become all you are meant to be.

Two-Way Connection

Then He said to the man, Reach out your hand. And the man
reached it out and it was restored, as sound as the other one.
MATTHEW 12:13 AMPC

This abiding in My presence, this tie between you and Me, is a two-way connection. When you need Me, when you want to connect to Me, when you appear before Me, you must make a move, take an action, reach out to Me with your hand. Only then, as you willingly put yourself toward Me, extend yourself to Me, can I touch you, restore you, make you whole.

So release yourself from all the worries and stresses that restrain your arms, that tie you down, that tether you, that keep you from experiencing the freedom you can find only in Me. At the same time, know that I am forever extending Myself, stretching Myself toward you, constantly, consistently seeking you, your presence, face, voice, spirit, and heart.

And when we connect—when we are both in this way aligned with each other, Father God, and His will—then you truly become My brother, sister, mother, part of My eternal family in light and love.

And stretching out His hand toward [not only the twelve disciples but all] His
adherents, He said, Here are My mother and My brothers. For whoever does
the will of My Father in heaven is My brother and sister and mother!
MATTHEW 12:49–50 AMPC

The Secret Place

*He who dwells in the secret place of the Most High shall remain stable and fixed under
the shadow of the Almighty [Whose power no foe can withstand]. I will say of the Lord, He is
my Refuge and my Fortress, my God; on Him I lean and rely, and in Him I [confidently] trust!*
PSALM 91:1–2 AMPC

I have promised you deliverance from the snares life can set. I have promised to cover you with
My wings, to lift you up to a place of refuge and protection, to defend you from evil and give My
angels charge over you, to lift you up from the cares of life and its issues so that you won't trip up
and fall upon your path. But you have yet to take advantage of all this.

Do so today and every day, in this moment and all the moments to follow. Come and abide in
Me. Dwell in the secret place, the one I have fashioned and reserved just for you. Here you can be
steady and focused. Here you can breathe freely. Here no power can touch you. Believe that I am
your shelter in the storm. Your high place above your earthly cares. I surround you with rock-solid
walls of protection, walls no one can breach.

Trust Me. Be confident in all I offer, all I provide. Rely, lean back upon Me. I've got you and
will never let you go. I am your secret place.

Timeless Message

Every part of Scripture is God-breathed and useful one way or another—showing us truth, exposing our rebellion, correcting our mistakes, training us to live God's way. Through the Word we are put together and shaped up for the tasks God has for us.

2 Timothy 3:16–17 MSG

Yes, I am the Ancient of Days. But do not think that because of My "age," I and My truths are irrelevant to you and your life, your world. For within My presence and My Word you will connect to and find the timeless wisdom of the ages.

With Me, you will find light for your path, direction for every avenue you take. You will find love surrounding you during good times and trials. You will find peace amid problems, comfort amid sorrow, courage amid discouragement.

There is no other place you can go to receive all that My Word and I provide. So come. Receive all that I have to offer, all that I am aching to share. Allow My wisdom to reshape you—and your world. Seek My presence and find your eternal purpose. And in following that purpose, that plan I laid out for you thousands of years ago, you will find your passion for this present.

My message to you is timeless. My way of life for you is eternal. Seek Me above all else.

Tailored for You

*The steps of a [good] man are directed and established by the Lord when He delights
in his way [and He busies Himself with his every step]. Though he falls, he shall not
be utterly cast down, for the Lord grasps his hand in support and upholds him.*
PSALM 37:23–24 AMPC

Connect with Me. Become more and more aware of My presence, My movement in your life every day.

Within this base of strength and power, move out to new challenges. Leave the regrets of the past behind. Do not fret about the future. Simply take what I am giving you, the nurturing aspects of My presence, and know that nothing can stand in your way when you abide in Me.

Take every situation you encounter as a kind of parable whereby I am speaking to you, sending you a message, revealing to you a valuable idea or tenet, tailored for you and your walk alone. I am attuned to your every step and your every breath. For I am in each.

So neither fear nor falter. I am holding you up. And because My hand is grasping yours, there's no way you will fall flat on your face. This special bond we share, this connection we have, is what will give you all that you need to walk the narrow way—with Me and all who have gone before, all who are cheering you on, even now.

Move Ahead

"Flee for your lives! Don't look back, and don't stop anywhere in the plain! Flee to the mountains or you will be swept away!"
GENESIS 19:17 NIV

You are worried about so many things outside your control—people, places, things, government, powers within and without, even your own self. Your mind stays on choices you made in the past and now regret. Your eyes cannot stop lingering on what you possess in the present. And so you hesitate, you stagnate, become stiff, and you miss all that I have set before you.

Know that I am the answer to all things that clamor to claim you. I am the power that can help you rise above all things. But you must listen. You must look. You must choose to obey Me. For only then can your soul truly grow, minute by minute, day by day, until one day you find joy beyond believing.

Do not be as Lot who, because of his hesitation to follow, had to be dragged out of his present situation. Nor be like Lot's wife who, because she could not stop yearning for what she'd left behind, could not go forward and so became a pillar of salt where she stood.

Instead of being swept away or destroyed in your inertia, move out in confidence with Me. Thrust your hand in Mine, with an eager willingness to be off and doing and being. Know that I have already equipped you with what you need to step forward. Live and move ahead in Me.

Grandeur of His Presence

"But ask the animals, and they will teach you, or the birds in the sky, and they will tell you; or speak to the earth, and it will teach you, or let the fish in the sea inform you. Which of all these does not know that the hand of the LORD has done this? In his hand is the life of every creature and the breath of all mankind."

JOB 12:7–10 NIV

I created nature not only to provide for and sustain you but to lift you up out of yourself. To remind you of the glory that is in Me. To show you that I am greater and more powerful and pleasurable than any worries or fears nipping at your resolve to live a holy life, a life rich in abundance, courage, steadfastness, and peace.

Meet Me in the nature that surrounds you. Walk with Me in the grandeur of My presence. See My nurturing in every leaf, My reflection in a river's surface, and My laughter and joy in the bird's song. See My creativity in the flower's shape, smell, color, and texture. My playfulness in the odd-shaped clouds. My glory in the sunrise. My peace in the sunset.

Do not neglect the relief you can receive from the gift of nature I have bestowed upon you. Walk with Me outdoors and lift your spirit up with Mine. As you do so, you will find many other doors opening in other areas of your life and walk.

Keeping the Peace

Your personal convictions [on such matters]—exercise [them] as in God's presence,
keeping them to yourself [striving only to know the truth and obey His will].
Blessed (happy, to be envied) is he who has no reason to judge himself for what
he approves [who does not convict himself by what he chooses to do].
ROMANS 14:22 AMPC

Do not be anxious when others view your actions as wrong. Nor force your own opinions about correctness onto others. I will make all things clear to you and for you in your particular life and circumstance.

The more time you spend with Me, the less anxious you will be about what is right and wrong, what is approved or not approved by Me. And the less you will be inclined to judge others and their own behavior.

Whatever you decide is right, keep it between Me and you. For your evident disapproval will not only disturb and upset others but trip them up in their walk with Me. Just stay true to your own convictions and keep the peace by being silent about them. By taking such a task, you will be acting in love *and* extending My kingdom, all to the glory of Father God!

So let's stop condemning each other. Decide instead to live in such a
way that you will not cause another believer to stumble and fall.
ROMANS 14:13 NLT

No Matter What

God is our refuge and strength, always ready to help in times of trouble. So we will not fear when earthquakes come and the mountains crumble into the sea. Let the oceans roar and foam. Let the mountains tremble as the waters surge!
PSALM 46:1–3 NLT

———◦◆◦———

If you are not yet continually abiding in My presence, may I be the first face you turn to in the time of storm and trouble, of earthquake and flood. Later, when you have reached a point where you are constantly abiding in My presence, any and all fear will be a nonissue. No matter what happens in your life, you will not be shaken.

Consistently abiding in Me takes much practice and patience. But the more quality time you spend with Me, the less you will worry and the more you will have peace of mind and courage.

For now, as you practice your abiding, be as gentle with yourself as I am and always will be with you. Begin with abiding for one moment each day until I become a habit you cannot do without. Then each day that follows, build upon those moments. By setting and maintaining such a course, you will find that I have become a natural ark for you, one in which you can ride in and above every storm you encounter.

For now, do not fear. I've got you. I will keep you safe and strong no matter what.

Inexhaustible Abundance

"I am the Gate. Anyone who goes through me will be cared for—will freely go in and out, and find pasture. A thief is only there to steal and kill and destroy. I came so they can have real and eternal life, more and better life than they ever dreamed of."
JOHN 10:9–10 MSG

I have never-ending patience, encouragement, grace, mercy, and love waiting for you. There is no way you can exhaust My supply of any good thing. I have all the resources you need at My command. So put away those frowns. Release all the limitations you have set upon yourself.

You are with Me now. Here you will find everything you need to live the life I have equipped you for, to do all that I have sent you and purposed you for. Once you make this fact a truth in your life and trust its meaning, all your anxieties will either go away completely or be very short-lived.

Believe Me in this. Your life lived in Me will be more satisfying and richer than you ever imagined. Test Me in this not by just being still in Me but by doing what I have called you to do. Take a step today toward a new beginning with this new confidence. Come to Me whenever you feel a shortfall in your needs. I will continually replenish you until you find yourself overflowing with all that you need—and more.

Unspeakable Yearnings

So too the [Holy] Spirit comes to our aid and bears us up in our weakness;
for we do not know what prayer to offer nor how to offer it worthily as we ought,
but the Spirit Himself goes to meet our supplication and pleads in our behalf
with unspeakable yearnings and groanings too deep for utterance.
ROMANS 8:26 AMPC

Come away with Me, out of the darkness of your worldly woes and into the sunshine of My presence. Leave the cave dwelling, the false sense of security, behind and stay with Me in this higher place of true safety, peace, and rest. Here you can bask in the warmth of My unconditional love. Feel My light upon your face. Relax upon the shores of My grace. And rest your weary frame, the one you've been trying to power in your own efforts, in your own energy and strength.

In Me, you will find rest for your soul. In Me, you will discover the calm of My silence. For between us no words need to be spoken. For together we have a language all our own.

Do not seek so much from Me in spoken words. Instead receive My touch as I consider your sigh. Imbue yourself in our union. Spirit to spirit. Soul to soul. Breath to breath. The richness found in our joining is a blessing to both, like no other.

Welcome In

Do not let your hearts be troubled (distressed, agitated). You believe in and adhere to and trust in and rely on God; believe in and adhere to and trust in and rely also on Me. In My Father's house there are many dwelling places (homes). If it were not so, I would have told you; for I am going away to prepare a place for you.
JOHN 14:1–2 AMPC

There is a place reserved for you. A place with Me. But your anxieties, your worries, your fears keep you at a distance, on the other side of the door. The weight of burdens you were never meant to bear is pulling you back, farther away from Me.

Drop all that hinders you. Just where you stand, let go of all that is weighing you down. Feel the ease that gives you, the unexpected lightness in your step, body, mind, spirit, and soul.

Now walk to My house. Open the door. Let us sit here together, comfortable in each other's presence, chatting about everything, sometimes ending each other's sentences, sometimes sitting in companionable silence, just blessed, content in each other's presence. Welcome in. Welcome home. Stay awhile.

And when (if) I go and make ready a place for you, I will come back again and will take you to Myself, that where I am you may be also. And [to the place] where I am going, you know the way.
JOHN 14:3–4 AMPC

The Circle of Love

Those who love God must also love their fellow believers.
1 John 4:21 NLT

Do not see people as you wish they would be. See them as they truly are, using the eyes of love. Such vision would be a blessing—and a continuation of the way I look at you. I take on all your mistakes, errors in judgment, slights, missteps, issues. Once I have pulled those layers away, once I can see past all those things, I get down to the heart of the matter—the love that is at the core of every human creature, the one thing that contains the most powerful energy in all creation. For God is love. And when you are able to see all things with His perspective, there is no room, no vision for anything else.

God loved you. So He sent Me, your Beloved, enabling you to face God with total confidence because you are following My example. Now when He looks at you, He sees perfect love, and all things come full circle. For when you are living in His love, you are living in God, and God lives in you. And there is no more fear. For that perfect circle of love has expelled all apprehensions, all dread of punishment.

Praise God for My love. Live in His love. And love all those you meet. The more you do, the more of God you will see in your world.

True Riches

Let the lowly brother glory in his exaltation, but the rich in his humiliation, because as a flower of the field he will pass away.

JAMES 1:9–10 NKJV

———◦•◦———

Be on the edge of your seat, in excited anticipation for not the worst that can happen in your life but the best I can provide you. Such preparation is needed to reap the blessings I have waiting in My hands for you.

This world has you so distracted, turning your head this way then that way, keeping you off balance, unprepared, unfocused, when I would have you standing steady, ready for the best, your eyes on Me.

Be more attracted to Me than distracted by the world. Look to Me; be focused on Me and what I have available to you, what I offer you each and every moment of the day. Loosen your grip on the world. Allow material things and temporal worries to fade away. Open yourself up to Me, ready to take on all the good I have to offer so that you will have the resources you need to walk forward, looking forward, unafraid because you know I am with you and in you. I am the giver of all good gifts—gifts that are uniquely yours and that are, through you, to be distributed to the world.

Look to Your Soil

"The seed that fell among the thorns represents those who hear God's word,
but all too quickly the message is crowded out by the worries
of this life and the lure of wealth, so no fruit is produced."
MATTHEW 13:22 NLT

Your heart is the soil I am looking to nurture with My Word so that you can become fruitful in all ways. Look to your grounding in My voice, My meaning, My Spirit.

Some allow the stones (troubles) in their soil (life) to prevent My Word from taking root. So where these seedlings first trusted in Me, they begin to fall away. Others allow thorns (worldly cares and love of money) to choke anything that's attempting to grow well so seedlings in this soil bear no fruit. Although they heard and loved what I told them, their troubles leave no room in their mind for the good words I imparted.

Look to have good soil. To truly hear and understand what My Word is telling you. When you do, you will find yourself growing taller and stronger, bearing more fruit than ever before, because you do so in spite of thorns and stones of this world. Praise God, the harvest you will produce for God's kingdom!

"The seed that fell on good soil represents those who truly hear and
understand God's word and produce a harvest of thirty, sixty,
or even a hundred times as much as had been planted!"
MATTHEW 13:23 NLT

The Better Way

The chariots of God are twenty thousand, even thousands upon thousands. The Lord is among them. . . . Blessed be the Lord, Who bears our burdens and carries us day by day, even the God Who is our salvation! Selah [pause, and calmly think of that]!
PSALM 68:17, 19 AMPC

Look to Me to carry you over all the troubles you are experiencing in your life. Trust that I have a better way—that I *am* a better way—of transportation. It is foolish to rely on earthy conveyances—things you can touch or see, like friends, money, a favorite preacher—to bring you up out of your troubles, out of yourself. Only I can truly help you find a way to rise above all the things that threaten to—and sometimes do—pull you down, away from Me and what I have to offer. I am your spiritual and earthly strength. I am your answer to whatever problems or troubles you face.

Because you seek Me within, I am your best vehicle into the heavenly realms where your peace and rest await. I will lift you high above the clouds and into the heavens, in this life and the next, where nothing can harm you. Where you can take the time to heal, to breathe, to rest, to gain a God-perspective. Where you can once again find all the strength you need—and more—to conquer!

Intimately Acquainted

[For my determined purpose is] that I may know Him [that I may progressively become more deeply and intimately acquainted with Him, perceiving and recognizing and understanding the wonders of His Person more strongly and more clearly], and that I may in that same way come to know the power outflowing from His resurrection [which it exerts over believers].
PHILIPPIANS 3:10 AMPC

Know Me more and more, becoming so familiar with Me that you are seeking a connection to Me in all things, all tasks, all people. Make this your purpose in life, going deeper and deeper with your spirit into Mine, coming closer and closer into the light of life. When you begin to understand why I have such a great love for you, you will find yourself reaching out to and loving others more and more in every aspect of your life, wanting to show them how to recognize Me as you do. And as you demonstrate your own love for Me, they too will want to know Me more and more, to see Me more clearly, and you will come to know, feel, and recognize My resurrection power. In this way, not only will your own power grow stronger each day, but you will be living your determined purpose, expanding God's kingdom, love, and light.

Girded with Strength and Power

The Lord reigns, He is clothed with majesty; the Lord is robed, He has girded Himself with strength and power; the world also is established, that it cannot be moved. . . . The Lord on high is mightier and more glorious than the noise of many waters, yes, than the mighty breakers and waves of the sea.

PSALM 93:1, 4 AMPC

I will be with you no matter where you are, no matter what you do, no matter when you do it. When all others desert you, when no one answers your cries for help, when there is no one to defend you, I will deliver you. I am your Savior in all ways, in all days.

When you dare to come out of the boat and the wind and waves threaten to consume you, to toss you about, all you need to do is call out to Me; I will be there that instant, reaching out, catching you, holding you before you go under.

No ocean storm, no matter how big its waves or how strong its wind, can sweep you out of My arms, can separate Me from you.

Know that I have clothed Myself with strength and power. I am mightier than any force in heaven or on earth. I am your ultimate defender, the victor over all foes, situations, and problems in your life. Trust Me in this. Prove Me in this.

Stand Your Ground

Be strong in the Lord [be empowered through your union with Him]; draw your strength from Him [that strength which His boundless might provides]. Put on God's whole armor [the armor of a heavy-armed soldier which God supplies], that you may be able successfully to stand up against [all] the strategies and the deceits of the devil.
EPHESIANS 6:10–11 AMPC

You are startled by so many things. Any disturbance in your plans and you become frustrated, are thrown off balance. Worse, you panic and either freeze, take fright, or fly.

Make it a practice to call on Me with every little care and concern, every interruption, mistake, or loss. Do not let your old ways come back into play, the ways you used to cope with fear, stress, or frustration. Instead, get armored up in My truth, peace, and Word. Know that your salvation and faith are your defense, the Holy Spirit your weapon. Be aware that even if it appears you've got far more than you can handle, that is not your true reality in Me. For your prayers, your persistence, your belief in Me and all that I have done, am doing, and will do in your life are where your true core power resides.

When you do all this, nothing will be able to shake you. You will be able to stand your ground with confidence and courage. You will overcome.

Incomparable Power

If you only look at us, you might well miss the brightness. We carry this
precious Message around in the unadorned clay pots of our ordinary lives.
That's to prevent anyone from confusing God's incomparable power with us.

2 CORINTHIANS 4:7 MSG

At times you may feel weak, discouraged, frightened, or distressed because of events and circumstances happening in your life. And that's okay. Just don't give in to those feelings. Don't lay yourself down and let them steamroll over you so that you're left flat—or worse, ineffectual for the kingdom. Instead, come to Me. Remember that when you are at your weakest, that's when I can shine the brightest! That's when you can become My best witness! People will marvel at the fact that because of My presence and power within you, you can endure any hardship, situation, or problem that you encounter. And you yourself will be amazed as well. For you will find you cannot come undone when I am holding you together. You will feel an amazingly potent supernatural power and strength streaming through you, enabling you to rise above anything the world can throw at you. And the more you trust in Me—the more you give way, the more rein you allow Me in your life—the more power will radiate from you, the more you will become like Me.

What-If vs. Who-Is

"Your father Abraham rejoiced as he looked forward to my coming. He saw it and was glad."
The people said, "You aren't even fifty years old. How can you say you have seen Abraham?"
Jesus answered, "I tell you the truth, before Abraham was even born, I AM!"
JOHN 8:56–58 NLT

While walking the earth, I told you that I AM. Believe this truth, this fact. For therein lies your strength, your power, your path. For so many are focused on the what-ifs of life. That is the place from which your anxieties and fears stem. The thoughts of *What if this or that happens? Then what will I do? How will I eat, live, love, work, play, find my way?* keep you from living the life I have planned out for you. Turn your focus from the what-if to *who-is*. Instead of wondering, *What if I weaken?* think, *Jesus is all the strength I need.* Change *What if I have already missed my chance?* to *Jesus is the door to all possibilities.* Replace *What if I can't do it?* with *Jesus is the one through whom I can do all things.* Substitute *What if I can't find my way, get lost in the dark?* with *Jesus is the Good Shepherd, the way, the truth, the life, and the light of the world.*

Know that I am the only definite thing in your life. I am the One who erases the what-ifs. I am the One WHO IS!

Kingdom Joy

Even though the fig trees have no blossoms, and there are no grapes on the vines; even though the olive crop fails, and the fields lie empty and barren; even though the flocks die in the fields, and the cattle barns are empty, yet I will rejoice in the LORD! I will be joyful in the God of my salvation!
HABAKKUK 3:17–18 NLT

My joy is available to you in the bleakest of circumstances. For I am working in all situations. What may look tenuous today will result in the strength of the ages tomorrow. What may look to be dying on the vine will find new life in another way.

Know that when you live to find joy in your walk with Me, the most amazing things begin to happen. Situations turn around. Your attitude, patience, outlook improve tenfold. Your joy becomes contagious to those around you. Contentment begins to take root and soon blossoms into confidence where before there was none.

Focus on the fact that I am—and will always be—with you in all ways and all days. I will care for and protect you. So do not worry. Let your cares drift away. For I am in control. I am witnessing all events. I see who is doing what. Leave all up to Me.

Your job is to focus on living in the kingdom of God—here and now! Exploring its riches. And serving your King. Rejoice in Me—the One who has saved you!

A Gift to Share

Stir up (rekindle the embers of, fan the flame of, and keep burning) the [gracious] gift
of God, [the inner fire] that is in you. . . . For God did not give us a spirit of timidity
(of cowardice, of craven and cringing and fawning fear), but [He has given us a spirit] of
power and of love and of calm and well-balanced mind and discipline and self-control.
2 TIMOTHY 1:6–7 AMPC

———◦•◦———

I have equipped you with certain desires and passions in the form of gifts. This is your reminder to use them. Let nothing deter you. For these gifts were given to you to enlarge the kingdom of God.

Whether you have the gift of wisdom, knowledge, faith, healing, miracles, prophecy, teaching, preaching, serving, leadership, pastoring, evangelizing, spiritual discernment, speaking, writing, working with your hands—practice it, use it. Do not worry if you *can* do it—*know* that you can. To whatever I have called you, I have also equipped you!

Allow neither fear nor nervousness to keep you from expressing the creative side of yourself, the part that is an aspect of the master Craftsman. You have been given a spirit of power, love, and discipline. Use it to express Me to the world, to allow Me to shine through you and reach others. Use your gift to enlighten, to enhance your life and the lives of those around you. Do not deny this gift or this spirit. But use them both to God's glory!

The Lord Appears

And the Angel of the Lord appeared to the woman and said to her, "Indeed now, you are barren and have borne no children, but you shall conceive and bear a son. . . ." The Angel of God came to the woman again as she was sitting in the field; but Manoah her husband was not with her.

JUDGES 13:3, 9 NKJV

My eyes see all things. My ears hear all your pleas. My heart knows your longings. My soul understands your circumstances.

I know your heartaches, and I come to relieve them, help you through them, resolve them. My Word stretches to span across the ages to touch your life, to speak into your life, even when you are doing nothing more than walking down the park path, driving down the road, sitting in a field.

You will hear My voice in your normal day-to-day situations and activities. Be aware that there is no expanse I cannot cross in time or place to help you find your way. Listen carefully when you are alone. Attune yourself to Me when you begin the humblest, the most routine of tasks, no matter where you are. Even if you are in a crowd of people, I can speak, I will speak, and you can hear if you will listen. Keep a door open for Me to work at all times. I will appear. I will guide. I will help.

Faith Always Rewarded

A woman who was a Canaanite from that district came out and, with a [loud, troublesomely urgent] cry, begged, Have mercy on me, O Lord, Son of David! . . . But He did not answer her a word. . . . But she came and, kneeling, worshiped Him and kept praying, Lord, help me!
MATTHEW 15:22–23, 25 AMPC

There may be days when you feel as if your faith is being tested. First you imagine I do not hear. Then you try to reason with Me. You may entertain the idea that I do not want to answer. Then you reconsider. You decide to reexamine exactly what you want then voice it to Me. Afterward, you may believe that I am walking away from you. Perhaps then you begin to not just plead with Me but worship Me, love Me, and continue praying.

Such faith, such persistence, humility, doggedness, patience, and perseverance in praying to Me is always rewarded. Allow seeming roadblocks, obstacles, discouragements to build up your faith, not tear it down! Know that I love you. I am waiting for you to come to a place where you will be ready for the answer I give you. This may take time. But, as you know, My timing is always perfect. And your faith always rewarded.

Then Jesus answered her, O woman, great is your faith!
Be it done for you as you wish.
MATTHEW 15:28 AMPC

Comforting Word

Joyful are those you. . .teach with your instructions. . . . Unless the LORD had been my help, my soul would soon have settled in silence. If I say, "My foot slips," Your mercy, O LORD, will hold me up. In the multitude of my anxieties within me, Your comforts delight my soul.
PSALM 94:12 NLT; PSALM 94:17–19 NKJV

Learn from My Word. Allow it to comfort you, soothe you, build you up so that when trials and troubles come your way, you will be more than able to stand against them. Your faith depends on it. Your walk requires it.

When you enter the world of My Word, allow it to speak to you, who you are, where you are. Do not depend so much on the words of other men to enlighten you. My Word can do that alone. That is its strength. That's how it has changed the world for thousands of years, has equipped many people of faith, and continues to do so today. My Word can change not only your life but the world.

And once you read it in its purest form, meditate on it. Ask Me what it means. I will rush to reply, to tell you how it applies to your life in such a personal way that you will know it was written just for you, in this moment, situation, particular point in time. Seek My Word and My presence. And amid all your worries and cares, I will soothe and bring joy to your soul.

The Provider

And God will generously provide all you need. Then you will always have everything you need and plenty left over to share with others. As the Scriptures say, "They share freely and give generously to the poor. Their good deeds will be remembered forever."
2 Corinthians 9:8–9 NLT

———◦◆◦———

You have all you need. I have promised that you will lack for nothing. Do not doubt this.

Look at the leaves on the trees, the sand on the seashore, the salt in the ocean. There is more than enough to provide for you and lots left over to help others in need.

I provide seed for the sower, yarn for the weaver, ink for the writer, paint for the painter, bricks for the mason. In the same way I sustain them, I will sustain you—and more besides! Not so that you can hoard your blessings, but so that you can take your extras to those who need them.

All is already yours. It is only a lack of faith that thinks otherwise. Take what little you have, even if it is faith as small as a mustard seed, and you can pull up a tree by the roots, plant it in the sea amid wind and waves. Believe in this and in Me. Believe that all you need has already been provided for. That it's just out there, waiting for you. Then reach for it and share it, spreading My goodness, My blessings where they have never reached before.

In His Love

The Lord your God is in the midst of you, a Mighty One, a Savior [Who saves]! He will rejoice
over you with joy; He will rest [in silent satisfaction] and in His love He will be silent and
make no mention [of past sins, or even recall them]; He will exult over you with singing.
ZEPHANIAH 3:17 AMPC

You are constantly on My mind. I adore you from break of day to the setting of the sun. While you sleep, I watch over you carefully. My arms ache to embrace you, cradle you, lift you, support you, and carry you. I tend to your needs and those of your loved ones. I do whatever I can to catch your attention, speak into your life, show you the paths you are to take. I counsel you, bless you with peace. I send you My angels to protect and encourage you.

See every generous act, every inspiration or cheer along the way, as a token of love, a sign of affection from Me. See every kind thought or deed as evidence that I am working in your life, looking to bring out not only the best in you but the best in all the lives that you touch.

Know My high regard for you and the lengths I will go to see that you are safe and sound.

I am in the midst of you, celebrating your triumphs, lifting you above trials, rejoicing over every little thing about you. See Me in love.

Rise Up

Now when Jesus had come into Peter's house, He saw his wife's
mother lying sick with a fever. So He touched her hand,
and the fever left her. And she arose and served them.
MATTHEW 8:14–15 NKJV

With one touch, I can make you well and whole. Feel My hand upon your body, My breath upon your spirit. Feel My all-encompassing love embrace your soul.

No long litany is needed for Me to remedy you. Just one look, one touch, one moment of contact, and the fever, the malady, the ache, the worry, the complaint, the sorrow, the need has left you. Then you are able to rise up and begin ministering to Me, serving Me.

Even now, thousands of years later, I am here. I see you. I am ready to touch you, to heal you, to make you whole, to rid you of all anxieties, fears, trepidations, and sadness, allowing relief, courage, confidence, and joy to enter in.

Have confidence that My healing powers are still so powerful, My methods so simple, My commitment to you so great. All I need is your faith as determined as Mine and My tender touch upon you to shed you of the physical weakness, the debilitating anxieties that weigh you down.

See Me; feel Me in this moment, touching you, healing you. And rise up in faith.

The Right Path

*"And we have believed in Christ Jesus, so that we might be made right with
God because of our faith in Christ, not because we have obeyed the law.
For no one will ever be made right with God by obeying the law."*

GALATIANS 2:16 NLT

———◦◆◦———

Relax. Let go of the things that are not serving you, the rituals that no longer draw you closer to Me but fill you with anxiety and angst and become tiresome, perhaps even irksome. Such things draw you away from, not closer to, Me. I have already freed you from all laws except for two: to love God with all of you and to love others as you love yourself. There is nothing more you need to do. No other formula you need to follow. Simply love. You have no other obligation.

Then to learn how to love Me more, know Me more, live more of who you are and are meant to be, yes, come to Me through the Word. Spend time in My presence through prayer. But have faith that in this regard I will lead you onto the path that is right for you. Follow Me, and Me alone, not some other's method or requirements. For then you will needlessly be worried if what you are doing "for Me" is enough.

Have faith. Look to Me for all I would have you do, for all I would have you be. Nothing more is needed, required, or necessary. Just turn to Me. Let's sit quietly. Let's begin there.

Pray

Pray at all times (on every occasion, in every season) in the Spirit, with all [manner of] prayer and entreaty. To that end keep alert and watch with strong purpose and perseverance, interceding in behalf of all the saints (God's consecrated people).

EPHESIANS 6:18 AMPC

———◦◆◦———

Come to Me. Speak to Me about everything. Pray all the time. I am here to help you every step of the way, every moment of the day. I want to hear all your cares. I want to hear all your requests, wishes, goals, and plans. For only then will I be able to help you find clarity, find your true path, to help you discover what you truly desire.

The more I went to My Father, the more relief and release I felt, just being in His presence, just telling Him all that was on My mind. I shared with Him My victories, sorrows, joys, and obstacles. That time alone was what refreshed, restored, and strengthened Me so that I could better serve Him and the ones I love.

The same goes for you. The more time you spend with Me, the wider God's kingdom of love can spread through you and around you. The more you will find the strength to serve and increase the power of your faith.

Do not neglect these most important and rewarding times alone with Me, no matter where you are or whom you are with. Nothing can separate us from each other. Nothing. Pray.

Let's Walk

So now there is no condemnation for those who belong to Christ Jesus.
And because you belong to him, the power of the life-giving Spirit
has freed you from the power of sin that leads to death.

ROMANS 8:1–2 NLT

Never think that because you have fallen in your walk that you have failed Me—or failed period. Such a mind-set will only keep you from getting up and continuing on the path that has been laid out for you. So take a moment—or two, if need be—to gather yourself. Take a quick inventory of where you tripped and what has been injured. Then brush yourself off and begin walking again.

Know that you are not alone. I am by your side, the Spirit is within, and God surrounds you. The only way you can fail is to become frustrated, lose your temper, and then give up. To allow the enemy to whisper in your ear, "You have failed. Stay down. No use getting up now."

Do not believe the accuser. Believe in Me—your Savior. Know that I have overcome him and the world. And I am working with you. I will help you stand. Just reach out your hand. I will pick you up, set you on your feet, support you until you are ready to walk again with Me, in the light of life and love, in the power of the Spirit that is operating within you right now. Feel Him. Feel Me. Let's walk.

Simply Trust

*[Urged on] by faith Abraham, when he was called, obeyed and went forth to a place which he
was destined to receive as an inheritance; and he went, although he did not know or trouble his
mind about where he was to go. [Prompted] by faith he dwelt as a temporary resident in the land
which was designated in the promise [of God, though he was like a stranger] in a strange country.*
HEBREWS 11:8–9 AMPC

Follow Me. Allow yourself to be spurred on by My promises. For the more you trust that I will do what I have said, that I will make real in your life what I have written in My Word, the further you will go, the more you will reap, the closer to Me you will get. You will begin to become the true you living the purpose for which you have been created. The more joy you will experience.

Go where I call you. Leave your fears and doubts, your anxieties and questions behind you. They have no place in the Promised Land. Do not trouble your mind about your specific destination. Do not worry if you don't know the exact next step. Simply trust that I know where you are going. That I will make what appears impossible possible. That I will make a way where there seems to be no way.

Simply cling to Me—and let Me take care of the rest.

A New Horizon

Let us kneel before the LORD our Maker. For He is our God, and we are the people of His pasture, and the sheep of His hand. Today, if you will hear His voice: "Do not harden your hearts, as in the rebellion, as in the day of trial in the wilderness."
PSALM 95:6–8 NKJV

So many times have I saved you from calamities, rescued you from dangers—seen and unseen—and pushed you out of harm's way. So many times I have blessed you beyond measure. I do all these things because I am your protector. I am the one who sustains you. I am your Good Shepherd. Yet I want to do more in your life. I want to bring you out into another broad place. I want to move you into position for great and delightful things. I have a marvelous plan, of which you are an integral part.

So keep yourself open. I am about to change some things up. And I want your ear. I want you to follow My voice, My words, My instructions. I want you to be attuned to all the ways I am moving in your life and the lives of others. For that, I desire your full attention, cooperation, and complete obedience.

Listen to Me as you have never listened before. Keep your heart open to My love, your mind open to My commands, and you will avoid the wilderness, the vast wasteland. Forget about any plans you might have. Allow Me to be your inner compass, your guide to a new horizon.

Great Transformations

*By faith these people overthrew kingdoms, ruled with justice, and received what
God had promised them. They shut the mouths of lions, quenched the flames of fire,
and escaped death by the edge of the sword. Their weakness was turned to strength.*
HEBREWS 11:33–34 NLT

Take whatever weaknesses you have and put them into My hands. There they can be transformed into something good, beautiful, strong, powerful, supernatural.

I have done it before. I can and will do it again. I took a hesitating Moses and made him a stalwart leader of the Israelites. I took a least-in-his-family Gideon and made him a judge of My people. I took Rahab the prostitute and made her a saver of spies. I took a young shepherd boy and made him not only a giant killer but a king. I took a woman-chaser named Samson, when he was seemingly shorn of his strength, and had him topple a huge building.

Imagine what I can do in your life. Consider the possibilities of what I can do in spite of or even through your perceived weaknesses. Put all those ways in which you feel feeble, in which you have tripped up before, into My hands. Let Me reform, remold, rework them into something that will serve not only you but My Kingdom work.

A Wholehearted Following

"But because my servant Caleb has a different spirit and follows me wholeheartedly,
I will bring him into the land he went to, and his descendants will inherit it."
NUMBERS 14:24 NIV

When you give up everything—everything you have, are, and hope to be—into My hands, amazing things happen. But it *has* to be *everything*, every part of you. In your walk with Me, it must be a wholehearted following on *your* part. That's what enables Me to do the *most* on *My* part.

You must believe that I will not mislead you, that I have the best plan for you. That may mean going against the ideas of others, including those you love. It means you must respect Me and My opinion above anyone else's—including your own. It means never giving up, no matter how bleak things look or how long you've been wandering the wilderness. It means hoping against hope. It means trusting that I will bring you into a good place, no matter how long it takes. It means believing that what I say is the true reality regardless of what your senses are telling you.

But it also means leading and living a life that I will enrich way beyond your imagination. You will see and take part in wonders. You will gain a treasure that can be passed down to those who come afterward.

Limited Vision

Samson told his father, "Get her for me! She looks good to me." His father and mother didn't realize the LORD was at work in this, creating an opportunity to work against the Philistines, who ruled over Israel at that time.
JUDGES 14:3–4 NLT

Don't worry about a thing. I've got a master plan. I'm working things out in ways you never would dream or imagine. Even the seemingly "bad" decisions of someone you love can be, in My hands, reformed, reshaped into something good.

Remember, I have a plan. A plan that you do not see in its entirety. A plan in which many people play many parts. There is no way you could grasp each cog in the wheel of life.

So relax. Know that I have a hand in everything. I am going to use each situation and each person's decision to work things out for the good. Granted, that which I "work out" may not turn out as you expected. But know and be assured that it will turn out in a way that will help further the kingdom of love and life to which you belong.

Thus, release all worries. Stand tall in your confidence in Me. Know that I am "at work" in all things, creating opportunities to spread the message, save My people, expand the Light, and enlarge the love.

The LORD directs the steps of the godly.
He delights in every detail of their lives.
PSALM 37:23 NLT

Delve into My Word

[Motivated] by faith he left Egypt behind him, being unawed and undismayed
by the wrath of the king; for he never flinched but held staunchly to his
purpose and endured steadfastly as one who gazed on Him Who is invisible.
HEBREWS 11:27 AMPC

⬧

Delve into My Word. Make it your mission to find the wisdom I have provided—just for you. Drench yourself in the words of Psalms. If you are uncertain about how to approach Me, if you cannot find the right words to say, use the psalms that continue to be sung to Me as conversation starters. Use scripture to communicate with Me, as I use it to communicate with you. There is so much power in that exercise.

Study the lives of the men and women who have walked the road of faith before you. There are so many examples for you to follow, so much wisdom to be gleaned, so many pitfalls to avoid.

Use My Word to increase your faith, to help you live unafraid of humankind, to keep you walking the road to which I have called you, to help you endure, to find Me—a treasure beyond compare.

I will meditate on Your precepts and have respect to
Your ways [the paths of life marked out by Your law].
PSALM 119:15 AMPC

Hand in Hand

"Don't panic. I'm with you. There's no need to fear for I'm your God.
I'll give you strength. I'll help you. I'll hold you steady, keep a firm grip on you."
ISAIAH 41:10 MSG

Picture us. Together. Crossing a street. You are just a child, your hand held firmly in Mine as we walk. The temperature is warm but the wind fierce, sounding, billowing around us. But with your hand in Mine, I am holding you steady. So steady that your feet barely touch the earth. It's as if you are dancing on air.

Your face wears a huge smile. In fact, you are giggling, your face turned toward the sky, your hair buffeted by the wind. Yet you don't care. You are taking joy in this moment. You are laughing at the wind. You are so secure in your connection with Me that you are not even aware of the possible dangers surrounding you. You know that I will keep all things in check. My eyes are ever open, watching, My body protecting. I am not just your companion but your champion.

Live your life in this manner. Walk with Me assured of My presence, of Me keeping you steady so that you can live without a care in the world. You know you are safe as you hold on to Me, as I guide you through the crossroads and beyond. I am your anchor in the winds of change, of adversity. What joy, what happiness you will experience.

Strength in Numbers

Two people are better off than one, for they can help each other succeed. If one person falls, the other can reach out and help. . . . A person standing alone can be attacked and defeated, but two can stand back-to-back and conquer. Three are even better, for a triple-braided cord is not easily broken.

ECCLESIASTES 4:9–10, 12 NLT

You are by no means alone. I have put people in your path to help you, to hold up your hands, to lessen your burden, to hone your strength. Neither neglect nor ignore them. For in doing so, you decrease the amount of power available to you.

I sent My disciples out two by two. I did this so that each person would have someone to hold him up if he fell. Father God provided Aaron for Moses, Ruth for Naomi, Jonathan for David. There is power in numbers. Especially when I join in, as I did for the two disciples who were walking on the road to Emmaus, trying to understand My parting from the world in physical form. I opened their eyes, made more things clear to them. I long to do the same for you and your companion.

Find someone to stand with you. Someone whom you can support and someone who can support you. When you are together, I will be there to strengthen you even further. Trust Me in this.

Well of Renewal

Samson was now very thirsty, and he cried out to the LORD, "You have accomplished this great victory by the strength of your servant. Must I now die of thirst and fall into the hands of these pagans?" So God caused water to gush out of a hollow in the ground at Lehi, and Samson was revived as he drank. Then he named that place "The Spring of the One Who Cried Out."
JUDGES 15:18–19 NLT

At times, you may forget that all victories you experience in your life are worked by *Me* through you. When you begin praising yourself instead of Me, I may send a bit of discomfort your way, something to jog your memory, to put things back into a God-perspective. Then when you cry out, I will answer in an amazing way, in a way you never even dreamed possible. I will revive you, replenish you, strengthen you, empower you once again.

I will hear your prayer—and glory in your praise. I will keep you sustained so that you do not fall back after a victory has been worked in your life. Know this. Remember who is always the ultimate deliverer. And look for refreshment, renewal, and revival around the corner of every triumph. Know that I will always be there to put a spring into your step, preparing you for the next challenge, the next opportunity to extend the kingdom of love and light.

Out of Your Heart

*"If you have faith as a mustard seed, you will say to this mountain,
'Move from here to there,' and it will move; and nothing will be impossible for you."*
MATTHEW 17:20 NKJV

My Word holds amazing, supernatural power. It is the kind of power that makes and breaks entire worlds, physical and spiritual. As one made in our Father God's image, you hold the same power with your own words. You must know this.

Therefore, be clear about this. You must watch your words. If you are afraid of what you will say in a certain situation or to a certain person, say nothing. If it is not to build up but to tear down, do not let a word pass your lips.

If you find yourself constantly having to stifle your words so as not to offend another soul, you may need to check your heart, the source of all words. Are you storing up good or bad treasure there? For it is out of your heart that your mouth speaks.

You are My follower. I have commanded you to love God, yourself, and others—in thought, word, and deed. So choose your words carefully. Think before you speak them. Make sure they are words of encouragement. Or speak not at all. For your words are too powerful to let them fly unstudied, unheeded, unholy. Best to let them remain unspoken.

Separating Fact from Fiction

The devil. . .was a murderer from the beginning and does not stand in the truth,
because there is no truth in him. When he speaks a falsehood, he speaks what is
natural to him, for he is a liar [himself] and the father of lies and of all that is false.
JOHN 8:44 AMPC

From the beginning, there has been one who has wanted to lead humankind astray. He comes in many forms and has been called by many names, mainly, the dragon, the devil, the serpent, or father of lies. And he continues to exist today, although he may now be craftier, subtler. He has woven himself intricately into the fabric of this world. Yet I have the power to defeat him. For I, who am in you, am greater than he who is in the world.

Be cautious. When doubts and questions arise, when your worries are more than you can bear, come to Me. Seek the truth of your thoughts, your attitudes, your emotions. Confide in Me, baring all that is in your heart and mind. Allow no barrier between us. And I will help you separate the fact (My truth) from fiction (the dragon's lies).

Be cautious. Allow no other voice to become louder or clearer than Mine. For I am the one who truly cares about you, knows what's best for you, and has the best for you in mind.

The Joys of Nature

*Let the heavens rejoice, and let the earth be glad; let the sea roar,
and all its fullness; let the field be joyful, and all that is in it.
Then all the trees of the woods will rejoice before the LORD.*
PSALM 96:11–13 NKJV

———◦◦◦———

Look around you. I am surrounding you with beauty—within and without. Come as My nature calls to you. Walk in My world. Breathe in its fullness.

Imagine My trees in the fall, their leaves bursting in reds, oranges, yellows, and browns. Imagine My flowers in the spring, each one taking on a different color, shade, hue, as individual as a fingerprint. Imagine My waterways, rivers, oceans, creeks, seas, each one teeming with life, providing for all creation.

Imagine all these things and take in the joy they exude. Let it flow deep into your heart. Put your focus on feeling that deep, deep joy until it gushes through your entire being and all anguish, angst, and anxiety is flooded away. Know that even during trials My joy is available to you. Simply seek Me out, cast your cares upon Me, and allow all My joy to overtake you. Till the joy of My nature is the joy of your nature.

....

....

....

....

....

....

....

....

*Now may the God of hope fill you with all joy and peace in believing,
that you may abound in hope by the power of the Holy Spirit.*
ROMANS 15:13 NKJV

Love and Acceptance

Therefore, accept each other just as Christ has accepted you
so that God will be given glory. . . . I am fully convinced,
my dear brothers and sisters, that you are full of goodness.
ROMANS 15:7, 14 NLT

Love yourself as I love you—just as you are. Love all the bumps and bruises, all the scars and scrapes. Love every part of your life—all that's working and all that isn't working. For all that you are and have is what I have given you, what I have blessed you with.

I also ask you to accept yourself as I have accepted you. Yes, there are areas in which you may be falling short. But those weaknesses are where I can reveal My greatest strengths, to show others that it is not by your power but by My power that you are becoming more and more a light to this world.

Only when you love and accept yourself can you truly love and accept all those around you. Only when you are aware of how many foibles you have, how My grace sees through them to the goodness that you are, can you too see that goodness in yourself and others.

Then the name of our Lord Jesus will be honored because of the way you live, and you will be honored
along with him. This is all made possible because of the grace of our God and Lord, Jesus Christ.
2 THESSALONIANS 1:12 NLT

Desired Outcomes

Roll your works upon the Lord [commit and trust them wholly to Him;
He will cause your thoughts to become agreeable to His will, and] so
shall your plans be established and succeed. The Lord has made everything
[to accommodate itself and contribute] to its own end and His own purpose.
PROVERBS 16:3–4 AMPC

Make a list of all the things on your plate today, then put them and their desired outcomes into My hands. Know that as I take care of you, I will take care of all things put in your charge.

So free your mind of all worries and cares. Know that as you work, I am working through you. I am conforming everything according to My will. So do not fret about the outcome of any endeavor, the plans of any day. However things work out, I will reshape the results to fulfill My purposes for you and the world.

Whatever you don't get done today, relax. Do it tomorrow. Know I am walking with you and My timing is always perfect. If a result was not what you expected, come and speak to Me. But leave My presence knowing I have a better way, a better idea, a better path. All is well. And the easier you rest in all this—the more you leave to Me—the more work will be done in accordance with My will and way. And the more peaceful you will become in all areas of life.

The Higher Things in Life

*If then you have been raised with Christ [to a new life, thus sharing His
resurrection from the dead], aim at and seek the [rich, eternal treasures] that
are above, where Christ is, seated at the right hand of God. And set your minds and
keep them set on what is above (the higher things), not on the things that are on the earth.*
COLOSSIANS 3:1–2 AMPC

Approach everything in your life with a calm assurance, knowing that I am in your midst, working everything out, protecting, guiding, and guarding every step of your path. Enter each endeavor with ease. Quietly hone your craft, improving yourself, your technique, and your knowledge in some way every day. When you do so, the peace I promise will rest within your heart, mind, body, spirit, and soul.

Know that any obstacle you come up against I can destroy or help you find your way around. Any battle that comes near you I will fight for you. Any harm or defeat you suffer I will turn into good.

Simply keep yourself above all strife and worry by setting your mind on all the good things, all the heavenly things. Rid your mind of the garbage of the lower world and fill your mind with such treasures of the higher world. Meet with Me often, through prayer, praise, and the Word. And most of all, thank Me for all that you have and are. With your focus on Me, things are looking up!

Meditating

*And Isaac went out to meditate and bow down [in prayer] in the open country in
the evening; and he looked up and saw that, behold, the camels were coming.*
GENESIS 24:63 AMPC

When you are worried, grieving, lonely, tired, confused, or wanting, do not delay. Come to Me. Run to Me. Seek Me out in an open field, a private room, a lonely beach, a hillside, a forest. I am waiting for you. I am yearning to hear your voice, to touch your life.

When you are stronger and ready for direction more than comfort, come into My Word, in prayer, looking for the light I am longing to give. I will bestow upon you all you need to go on—and more. I will give you the power to hang on, the patience to wait. And one day you will find yourself looking up and seeing better days, days filled with a joy and peace that you never anticipated.

All this is what I can do when you mediate on Me and My Word. When you show up where I've been waiting to greet you. Continually, calmly think on Me and My Word. I'm here. Waiting.

*This Book of the Law shall not depart out of your mouth, but you shall meditate on it day
and night, that you may observe and do according to all that is written in it. For then you
shall make your way prosperous, and then you shall deal wisely and have good success.*
JOSHUA 1:8 AMPC

Only This One

"By the name of Jesus Christ of Nazareth. . . by means of his name this man stands before you healthy and whole. . . . Salvation comes no other way; no other name has been or will be given to us by which we can be saved, only this one."
ACTS 4:10, 12 MSG

Trust in Me and Me alone. Not in riches. For they are here today and gone tomorrow. Not in material possessions. For those are things that moths and rust can destroy. Not in your fellow human beings. For their strength is limited. Not in your reputation. For it is fleeting and tenuous at best.

Only I can save you. Only I have the power to raise the dead. Only I love you enough to die for you so that you can be reconciled with Father God. Only I have enough compassion to forgive and forget all your sins.

Put all your hope in Me. For I am the only one who will never disappoint you. Instead I will equip, encourage, strengthen, empower, love, fortify, defend, protect, and fight for you. I am the One who walks with you in the fire, lifts you out of the pit, holds out a hand for you in the darkness. Only Me, only this one. Trust in, look to, hope in, and be saved by Me alone.

Light Walker

*Light is sown for the [uncompromisingly] righteous and strewn
along their pathway, and joy for the upright in heart [the irrepressible
joy which comes from consciousness of His favor and protection].*

PSALM 97:11 AMPC

———◦•◦———

You are a child of the Light because you follow and belong to Me. I am not only filling you with light but spreading it upon your pathway. The longer you walk, the closer you are to Me; the more light shines upon your path, keeping you clear of pitfalls, obstacles, and unseen dangers. Know this. Remember this. Do not allow doubt, confusion, anxieties, and fears to trip you up. When they come across your path or threaten to block you, simply draw closer to Me and soon you will again see the light. Your pathway will become brighter, your step surer, your walk unhindered once again.

Revel in the joy such a walk brings as you not only come, seek, and listen to Me but obey My instructions. Traveling beside such a Light walker, I will help you decide what is right and help you to make it happen.

Come. Shed the darkness of despair. Allow your cares to fade away. Feel My Son-light. Walk with Me and experience the joy in your heart!

....

....

....

....

....

....

....

....

*You're sons of Light, daughters of Day. . . . Walk out into the
daylight sober, dressed up in faith, love, and the hope of salvation.*

1 THESSALONIANS 5:5, 8 MSG

Move with Compassion

"The master of that servant was moved with compassion, released him,
and forgave him the debt. . . . 'Should you not also have had
compassion on your fellow servant, just as I had pity on you?'"
MATTHEW 18:27, 33 NKJV

I have shown you such compassion. I have loved you—and continue to love you—from the deep recesses of My heart. Because of My empathy toward and devotion to you, I gave My life. Because of that, your misdeeds are not only forgiven but forgotten. You have a clean slate, a new beginning each and every day.

Yet you have cares and worries within you. It may be that something is darkening your heart, keeping you from realizing the total joy you can find in Me, the total forgiveness you receive from Me only when you forgive others. Look within. Delve deep. Just as I have had compassion for and forgiven you, so must you have compassion for and forgive anyone who has ever slighted, hurt, or insulted you or someone you love. Loose the grudge you are holding. Let it go—not just from the mind but from your heart. Only then will your spirit be free to bask in the light, the amazing light, found in total forgiveness—from Me to you and from you to your brothers and sisters. Move with compassion from the darkness of bitterness and resentment into the light of love and forgiveness.

A New Song

*Sing a new song to the LORD, for he has done wonderful deeds. His right
hand has won a mighty victory; his holy arm has shown his saving power!*
PSALM 98:1 NLT

Each day that you walk with Me you find more and more knowledge and wisdom, experience and insight. For you are seeking Me in prayer. You are finding Me in praise. And most of all you are learning of Me through your study of the Word.

Each day you find something new in the scriptures. Something that you read several times before suddenly means something different, changes your game plan, leads you in a new direction, gives you a different insight. You cannot help but rejoice!

This is what it means to be living in the living Word. This is what it means to have the Spirit by your side, helping you to understand. This is what it means to be moving closer to God, being reshaped by your increasing knowledge of Him.

Sing a new song to Me! Tell Me what you have learned! Know you are closer and closer to something spectacular! Look upon Me and your life and our working together with fresh eyes. See the path I am laying before you, the promises that are coming to the fore, the victory that is within reach. Know that something wonderful is happening in your life.

Silent Waiting

*My soul, wait only upon God and silently submit to Him; for my hope
and expectation are from Him. He only is my Rock and my Salvation;
He is my Defense and my Fortress, I shall not be moved. . . . Trust in, lean on,
rely on, and have confidence in Him at all times. . .pour out your hearts before Him.*
PSALM 62:5–6, 8 AMPC

Wait upon Me. Come to Me in the silence. There you will find Me and the solace for your soul.

Be confident in Me, your Rock, your Savior, your protector. No matter what comes up against you, I am there to hold you up. Pour out your heart to Me. Empty your mind of all that is troubling you, giving you unrest. Wait in the silence. I am right beside you. We are breathing in rhythm. It is here that our minds connect. With your thoughts mingled with Mine, My wisdom moves through you, directing you, guiding you, advising you.

Continue here. Abide here. Wait here, on Me. Trust that I am with you, that you are safe and will remain so in My presence. Expect Me to speak—to inform, transform, and reform you. As I spoke to David, I am speaking to you. . .in the silence. . .as you wait. Pour out your heart. I'm listening.

Investing Time

"A nobleman was called away to a distant empire to be crowned king and then return. Before he left, he called together ten of his servants and divided among them ten pounds of silver, saying, 'Invest this for me while I am gone.'"
LUKE 19:12–13 NLT

Come. Rest in Me.

You are exhausted, trying to find enough time to do your heart's desire as well as take care of all those around you. How much anxiety this is causing you to suffer. Doing so much for others, your resentment begins to build. Soon your time with Me falls by the wayside when it should be that time that fuels you, re-centers you, nurtures you.

Stop trying to live this life in accordance with what you think you should be doing with your time. Instead, gain My perspective. You have been saved—not just from sin but from this world's demands on you. I did that for you on the cross. Yes, I have asked you to serve, but not to do so to the point where you lose Me in the process.

So come away with Me, here, now, in this moment. Know that I have saved you. Your life is eternal. There is no need to rush. No need to be so busy with to-dos for yourself and others that you forget to *be*—My love and light. Here and now, sit. Lean back against Me. Breathe. Know you have all the time in heaven and on earth—in Me. Ask Me what you should do next. And build your day from there.

Truly Right

In those days Israel had no king; all the people did whatever seemed
right in their own eyes. . . . So Micah's carved image was worshiped by
the tribe of Dan as long as the Tabernacle of God remained at Shiloh.
JUDGES 17:6; 18:31 NLT

Throughout the ages, it has been so easy for people to get caught up in what the world thinks is right and wrong. Even My followers did! They found fault in My words and actions—instead of finding fault within themselves. And still today, everyone gets caught up in doing what they think is right.

I would have you wake up. Know that I am your King—now and forever. I've given you all the precepts within My Word to save you from a life filled with anxiety, worry, fear, and shame and to help guide you, lead you to what is truly right.

Home in on My teachings alone—not on what those around you think is right. For if you aren't following Me, you are rejecting Me as King, as Lord over your life.

Check your heart. Determine who or what is reigning there, who or what you are truly worshipping. Dethrone that entity. Turn and follow Me. Do what is right in *My* eyes. And you will not only find rest for your soul but the pathway to eternal light and life.

Vital Union

Apart from Me [cut off from vital union with Me] you can do nothing. . . .
If you live in Me [abide vitally united to Me] and My words remain in you and
continue to live in your hearts, ask whatever you will, and it shall be done for you.
JOHN 15:5, 7 AMPC

Open My Word and feel its power move through you, soothing, lifting, teaching, loving. Settle into its rhythm. Immerse yourself in it. Let it flow through you. Allow it to slowly take root in your heart, spirit, soul, and mind, to become a part of you, your existence, your very being. Let it begin to lead your life, your every step, every word. Allow it to become the source of your strength, the nourishing and nurturing sap that flows through you, sustains you, remakes you. Grow into it, seeing something new there each passing day.

When you are living a life separate from Me, you will be waylaid by the worries and cares this world brings. They will suck the life out of you. But when you are living so close to Me that people cannot tell where you begin and I end, when people see you living My Word, then anything that you ask for will be done for you.

You choose where to live your life. Choose Me.

One Thing

Martha welcomed him into her home. Her sister,
Mary, sat at the Lord's feet, listening to what he taught.
But Martha was distracted by the big dinner she was preparing.
LUKE 10:38–40 NLT

———◦•◦———

Each day, find a quiet place where you and I can meet without being interrupted, even if it's only for a moment or two. For sometimes that is all I need to speak a good word, leave a vital direction in your mind, one you would otherwise miss in the busyness of your day.

Let all other distractions and commitments fade away. This is our time. A chance to commune, connect, converse. This is your time to relax, to sit back in silence or cry on My shoulder. This is your time to find the answer to a question that has been disturbing you for a while. This is your time to let the light with which I have filled you linger with and be rekindled by Mine. I long to fill you, teach you, advise you, help you. So, take this moment now. . .to sit directly at My feet. Lean up against My legs. Close your eyes and listen for and to My voice.

....

....

....

....

....

....

....

....

....

....

"My dear Martha, you are worried and upset over all these
details! There is only one thing worth being concerned about.
Mary has discovered it, and it will not be taken away from her."
LUKE 10:41–42 NLT

Creature Comforts

GOD arranged for a broad-leafed tree to spring up. It grew over Jonah to cool him off and get him out of his angry sulk. Jonah was pleased and enjoyed the shade. Life was looking up.
JONAH 4:6 MSG

Are you swayed by trifles?

A once-disobedient Jonah was angry when, in accordance with God's compassion, He didn't destroy a city full of disobeyers. So Jonah went outside the city to sulk. When it started to get hot, Father God provided a gourd to comfort him with shade. Finally, Jonah was happy—but that was short-lived. When God produced a worm to wither the gourd, then brought a hot wind to burn up Jonah's head, his anger took over once more.

Do not be like Jonah! Cease to murmur and complain! See all that you receive as a gift from My hand. Do not let every bad circumstance anger or dismay you. All your creature comforts will one day fade away. But that should be of no regard. For I will never fade. I will always be with you.

Focus on Me—the eternal. See how merciful I have been to you, how much I have provided you! See how much I have forgiven you! See how much I love you! Then go and do likewise, taking all the good with the bad, being My steady servant, swayed only by Me and not every trifle.

Your Calling

God knew what he was doing from the very beginning. He decided from the outset to shape the lives of those who love him along the same lines as the life of his Son.

ROMANS 8:29 MSG

———◦•◦———

Do not be anxious about the plans I have made for you. I have often used things considered small to do great things, called people to accomplish great purposes.

Aaron's rod turned Egypt's water to blood and summoned a mass of frogs on the land. Moses' rod defeated an army and brought water gushing out of a rock—twice! Joshua used trumpets and the shouts of people to bring down the wall of Jericho. Rahab's use of a red rope saved her and her family from annihilation.

God called David, a shepherd boy, to defeat a Philistine giant. He called a young girl to bear and give birth to Me, and a carpenter to be My earthly father. I Myself called mainly fishermen to be My disciples.

Now I am calling you. Great things are in store.

_____

_____

_____

_____

_____

_____

_____

_____

_____

After God made that decision of what his children should be like, he followed it up by calling people by name. After he called them by name, he set them on a solid basis with himself. And then, after getting them established, he stayed with them to the end, gloriously completing what he had begun.

ROMANS 8:30 MSG

A Second Time

Then the Lord spoke to Jonah a second time: "Get up and go."
Jonah 3:1–2 NLT

No matter where you are, know that I will never give up on you. No matter how many years you wander in the wilderness, no matter how many times you go around the mountain, I will never leave nor forsake you. I will continue to keep equipping you, supplying you, caring for you until you are ready to obey. Until you see the light.

I am the God of second chances. And as I give My mercy to you, as I continue to care for you until you are ready to walk the path I have laid out for you, give those in your life—loved ones who have gone astray or offended you in some way—second chances. Never close the door on them. Allow them a way back to you. For do I not do so for you?

And continue to be soft and gentle with yourself, as needed. Never close the door on the dreams you once held dear. Give them a second chance, a second try.

Use the lessons I continue to teach you—through My Word and your experiences—to find a way to persevere. I will help you. I will give you the strength to extend mercy, to never give up or surrender.

Forever Love

If I [can] speak in the tongues of men and [even] of angels, but have not love (that reasoning, intentional, spiritual devotion such as is inspired by God's love for and in us), I am only a noisy gong or a clanging cymbal.

1 CORINTHIANS 13:1 AMPC

In their sorrow, in their despair, many ask, "Where is love?"

Here is love. I am LOVE. I am the answer to every problem, every question, every care, every quandary. Turn to Me. Dwell in My love; drink it in. Allow it to flow into every sinew, every pore of your mind, body, heart, soul, and spirit. Allow it to saturate you and then overflow out onto others, pouring into the hearts of those you encounter.

I am love. You are My follower. Take this love, knowing that it tolerates anything that comes its way, believes the best in all people, has unfading hope no matter what's happening, and endures everything without losing its strength. Make loving others your mission in life. *Be My love. And gain love itself.*

....

....

....

....

....

....

....

....

....

....

Love is patient and kind. Love is not jealous or boastful or proud or rude. It does not demand its own way. It is not irritable, and it keeps no record of being wronged. . . . Love will last forever!

1 CORINTHIANS 13:4–5, 8 NLT

God Speaks

*"For God speaks again and again, though people do not
recognize it. He speaks in dreams, in visions of the night, when deep
sleep falls on people as they lie in their beds. He whispers in their ears."*
JOB 33:14–16 NLT

———○•◦○———

Pour out your heart before Me as you lie upon your bed at night and as you awaken in the morning. I will speak to you if you are open to Me—at dusk and daybreak, while awake or dreaming. If you will really listen, you will hear My whispers, My warnings.

I speak, and have spoken to you, over and over again. But sometimes you do not recognize it, you have not truly heard. Or you did not understand because you did not expect it.

Know that I will come to you, seek you out, reach out to you in many ways. As God reached out to men and women time and time again, He and I will do so again to you—if you are open, waiting, wanting, seeking. Think and meditate on these things. Then listen. Help is on its way.

....

....

....

....

....

....

....

....

....

*O God, you are my God; I earnestly search for you. My soul thirsts for you; my whole body
longs for you in this parched and weary land where there is no water. . . . I lie awake
thinking of you, meditating on you through the night. Because you are my helper.*
PSALM 63:1, 6–7 NLT

Kindness and Compassion

"When you help someone out, don't think about how it looks. Just do it—
quietly and unobtrusively. That is the way your God, who conceived
you in love, working behind the scenes, helps you out."
MATTHEW 6:3–4 MSG

A natural effect from experiencing the kindness and compassion I have for and give to you is the growing desire you have to be kind and compassionate to those around you. Do you not feel it? Do you not sense this?

And this is also what I have called you to do, to love others. When you do so, when you come out of being with Me and then move the next instant into prayerfully doing for Me, the rewards are a thousandfold. For you find yourself less stressed and anxious, more joyful and contented. As you do more and more for others, you will become an impassioned conduit of all that is good and right—regardless of whether you are thanked, the accolades from others, or even whether the one who received your goodness is aware of you being the giver. This is how I would have it be. This is how I have worked it out in this life.

Whether you do your deeds in secret or not, do them, regardless of how you feel mentally or emotionally—and you will benefit not only others but yourself as you move from a self-focus to a loving-others focus.

Who I Am

Jesus. . .asked his disciples, "Who do people say that the Son of Man is?" "Well,"
they replied, "some say John the Baptist, some say Elijah, and others say Jeremiah
or one of the other prophets." Then he asked them, "But who do you say I am?"
Simon Peter answered, "You are the Messiah, the Son of the living God."
MATTHEW 16:13–16 NLT

I am the Son of the God who lives, the One who has saved you, the One who is your mediator between you and the Father. I am your teacher, training you up in the way you should go. I am mighty, compassionate, perfect. Holy, righteous, reliable, and good. I can heal, protect, empower, and restore.

Think on all these things, on all that I am, on all that I do, and your fears and worries will vanish. For I am all that you could ever need or desire. I am love personified. I am kind, caring, and infallible. When you cry, I respond. When you laugh, I partake of joy with you. When you need help, I move immediately.

I am your inspiration, the One you often turn to when you come to the end of yourself. I am mightier than any force that can come against you. I will deliver you from all that hinders you.

Believe this. Reflect on this. Know Me, and live.

Soul Expectations

For God alone my soul waits in silence; from Him comes my salvation. . . . My soul,
wait only upon God and silently submit to Him; for my hope and expectation are from Him.
PSALM 62:1, 5 AMPC

Place your hope in Me alone. Do not base your expectations on other people's words or deeds. For if you look to others to meet all your expectations, you are bound to be disappointed, aggrieved, frustrated. Other people or things have not been created to fulfill your every dream and hope. I alone can meet that need, that desire, that urge. I alone am your joy and expectation.

For only I can love and forgive you unconditionally, can give you the power to move mountains, the strength to conquer the forces that come up against you. Only I can give you light in the darkness, hope for tomorrow, comfort for today. My resources for you are unlimited. My knowledge of you unbounded.

I alone can lift you above the waters, save you from the fires, shield you from the sun, hear your inner cries for understanding and compassion. Only I can heal your mind, body, spirit, and soul. Only I can give you the confidence and focus to walk on the waters during a raging storm. Only I can bring your boat into a safe port. Know this. Expect this—from Me and no other.

Proud Waves

"Or who shut in the sea with doors, when it burst forth and issued from the womb. . .
when I fixed My limit for it, and set bars and doors; when I said, 'This far you
may come, but no farther, and here your proud waves must stop!' "
JOB 38:8, 10–11 NKJV

Only I control the wind and the waves. Only I call the dawn and bring in the night. Only I keep this world turning on its axis. Only I control and have overcome all things.

Do not confuse yourself with Me. Do not attempt to control yourself or those around you. For such attempts will lead only to sorrow or frustration.

Leave all things in My hands. Know that I have a plan, that I am working everything out. Recognize that I alone hold the power to bring all things to a good end or beginning.

Curb your anxieties by letting go of the need, the desire to control. Allow that pressure to command the uncontrollable to roll off your shoulders. Allow the tendency to force things and others to weaken. Relax in the joy of filling your soul and spirit with the true faith, love, and light that can move more mountains, change more hearts, than any other human power on earth. And let Me take care of everything and everyone else. Feel what ease this gives you, what new life this bestows on you.

Plans, Solid and Sure

*G*OD*, you are my God. I celebrate you. I praise you. You've done your*
share of miracle-wonders, well-thought-out plans, solid and sure.
ISAIAH 25:1 MSG

Beware of allowing other people's ideas, notions, and opinions to keep you from walking the path I have laid out for you. Who better than I knows what you are fit for? Who better than I knows that the time is right, the time is yours?

Have I not had you in mind from the very beginning, before you were even formed in your mother's womb? Did I not save you, love you, before you even knew who I was?

Do not let those who consider themselves "worldly wise" give you pause. Instead, look to Me for all wisdom. Delve into Me—the Word and Light of life. Know that I am holding all the answers you need; you simply need to seek them. Relax in that knowledge. Walk assured of My presence and guidance. Stand steady in My strength, no matter how strong the words of others beg you to turn aside. Rest in the plans I have made for you. And love, in My name, all whom you encounter.

Live your purpose—to obey Me, follow Me. I've already gone ahead and cleared the way. Your task is to focus on taking one step after another, continuing on the path I have laid before you.

Under His Hand

Know (perceive, recognize, and understand with approval) that the Lord is God!
It is He Who has made us, not we ourselves [and we are His]!
We are His people and the sheep of His pasture.
PSALM 100:3 AMPC

You take too much upon yourself when you begin thinking that you are a self-made woman. What pressure you must feel under, to get it just right. You are taking on My responsibilities, My challenges, My sense of perfection. You deserve neither censure nor credit for what and who you are! You fail to remember that it's not all about you—it's all about Me!

I am the God who heals you, calls you, forms you, and reshapes you. I am the potter—you are the clay! So just lie down on My wheel. Keep still before Me. Allow Me to remake you into the unique vessel I have already envisioned you to be. Let Me form and shape you, test you, fire you, and glaze you. The less pliable you are under My hand, the longer it will take to fashion you into the perfect creature I have planned you to be.

Let's begin now, today. Set aside all preconceptions, all current conditions, all worries about what has been, is, and will be. Be still. Relax. Settle here beneath the palms of My hands. Feel their warmth. Their gentleness. Leave all up to Me. I've got you in My hands. All is well.

Enoughness

Look at the birds of the air; they neither sow nor reap nor gather into barns,
and yet your heavenly Father keeps feeding them. Are you not worth much more than
they? And who of you by worrying and being anxious can add one unit of measure
(cubit) to his stature or to the span of his life? And why should you be anxious. . . ?
MATTHEW 6:26–28 AMPC

Stave off any worries about enoughness. Know that in the unseen realm, I am providing for, planning for, your future supply. And current supplies are already on their way to your doorstep.

Your weapon against this type of worry is faith. Faith that I love you and want the best for you. Faith that there is something awaiting you, something not just good but wonderful. Faith that I am more concerned with you than any other creature.

Build up your faith by being still before Me, spending time in My Word, meditating on My promises, singing My psalms. The more faith you build up—the more faith you have that I love you and will provide for you—the less you will worry. And the less you worry, the more you will find the passion, time, and energy to live the life for which I have prepared you.

Trust Me in this. I will more than provide. Believe this today, and you will have your supply tomorrow.

A New Thing

Thus says the LORD. . ."Do not remember the former things, nor consider the things of old. Behold, I will do a new thing, now it shall spring forth; shall you not know it? I will even make a road in the wilderness and rivers in the desert."
ISAIAH 43:16, 18–19 NKJV

Do not fret about the errors you have made, the misjudgments, the missteps. Those things are what make you uniquely you. Those mistakes are what make you the exact person I need to do what I have planned for you to do.

Mistakes keep you humble, compassionate, and soulful. In My hands, they are re-created into something new, something beneficial to you or others. Cease your ruminating over them, wondering what your life or world would be like if you'd made a different choice. That time is over. Look away. Look to Me. Right now I am doing a new thing.

So do not dwell, do not linger on the past. Move out into the expanse I have created for you to find, fill, and fuel. Stick close to My side. I will keep you on the better path. I will show you a better way.

Learn from the past. Then leave it behind. Put your hand in Mine. Walk with Me into the new world that awaits you, a new mind-set, a new adventure, a new day.

Ready and Waiting

So Jesus stood still and called them, and said, "What do you want Me to do for you?"
They said to Him, "Lord, that our eyes may be opened." So Jesus had compassion and
touched their eyes. And immediately their eyes received sight, and they followed Him.
MATTHEW 20:32–34 NKJV

Every morning I come to you and ask, "What do you want Me to do for you?" But oftentimes, your mind is filled with so many cares and woes, so many what-ifs, that you do not hear. You do not see Me—ready and waiting for you to turn to Me, to acknowledge Me, My power, My longing to work in your life.

On this day, in this moment, let all your worries subside. Think about Me and My will for your life. Search your heart. Then ponder: "What do you want Me to do for you?"

What do you want? What does your heart desire? Answer these questions; put those desires before Me. Then trust Me to provide for you—regardless of what other people think or say. Turn from the voices of the discouragers and turn to Me, the Encourager. I am still here before you, calling to you, wanting you to embark on the pathway already prepared for you. I have compassion toward you, only good in mind for you. I will touch you. I will give you the sight you need to follow Me. What do you want Me to do for you?

A Pattern to Follow

Therefore be imitators of God as dear children. And walk in love,
as Christ also has loved us and given Himself for us, an offering
and a sacrifice to God for a sweet-smelling aroma.
EPHESIANS 5:1–2 NKJV

Pause. . . . Pray. . . . Praise. . . . Ponder My words. Do not just skim over them but pause, pray, praise, and ponder.

Be. . .ye. . .therefore. . .followers. . .of. . .God. . . . As. . .dear. . .children. . . . And. . .walk. . .in . . .love. . . . Be. . .followers. . . .

Let these words sink into your very core. Let them fill your entire being with the light I have brought into the world. Recognize their saving power, rescuing you from worries, bitterness, angst, trauma, and grief. Know that I have left you a pattern to follow, a course that can guide you through all aspects of life. You have already embarked upon that course. But you must follow it steadily, hand in hand with Me. Go deep into My Word, your road map. Pause as you read it. Pray what soothes your heart. Praise Me for its empowerment of you. Then make it part of you and your life by pondering some aspect of it throughout the day. Do not stray from its promises and power. Dear child, follow God. Imitate Me. I will lead you to the kingdom of God—on earth and in heaven. Pause. . . . Pray. . . . Praise. . . . Ponder.

Expectant Faith

Now faith is the assurance (the confirmation, the title deed) of the things
[we] hope for, being the proof of things [we] do not see and the conviction
of their reality [faith perceiving as real fact what is not revealed to the senses].
HEBREWS 11:1 AMPC

Your joy lies in your faith, your expecting that what Father God and I have promised is and will become your reality. It will be performed in your life—regardless of the apparent physical "evidence" around you. Know that the things you hope for—the things you cannot see, touch, taste, hear, or smell—exist. Be convinced of that spiritual reality. Live your life with that assurance. In this way, you will not only have joy unsurmountable but be blessed in all aspects of your life.

Come near to Me in this moment. Reach out to Me, spirit to Spirit. Rest in that supernatural knowing that I am real. Touch My hands and My feet. Feel the love they represent.

Know that no one loves you more than I. Believe. Expect. And be blessed.

But without faith it is impossible to please and be satisfactory to Him. For whoever
would come near to God must [necessarily] believe that God exists and that He
is the rewarder of those who earnestly and diligently seek Him [out].
HEBREWS 11:6 AMPC

Your Right Arm

O Lord, be gracious to us; we have waited [expectantly] for You. Be the arm [of Your servants—their strength and defense] every morning, our salvation in the time of trouble.

ISAIAH 33:2 AMPC

———◦•◦———

Smile. Feel My love. The joy of My salvation. The freedom granted you in My burden bearing.

I have heard your pleas. I have seen your circumstances. As expected, I am here to give you the strength you need to face this day. I am your power. I am the One who defends you.

Do not allow the worries of your mind, the fears of your heart, the maladies of your body, the injuries to your soul, the discouragement of your spirit to overcome you. I have had victory over all so that you too are a conqueror.

So, begin your morning with a mind filled with promises, a heart of faith, a body of health, a soul of healing, and a spirit of courage. I am empowering you. I am your right arm. I will shield you from all that comes against you. You have waited. I am here. Now, open up and let Me work. Do not delay. Know that nothing can stand against you. For there is nothing mightier, stronger, more powerful than Me, your Savior. Now rise up.

Fulfilled

"He sent from above, He took me, He drew me out of many waters. He delivered me from my strong enemy. . . . The LORD was my support. He also brought me out into a broad place; He delivered me because He delighted in me. . . . God is my strength and power, and He makes my way perfect."
2 SAMUEL 22:17–20, 33 NKJV

Turn to Me. Relax. Let Me lift you up, draw you above and into My embrace. You are safe here in the shelter of My arms. No one and nothing can hurt you when You are abiding in Me. I will hold you, nurture you, until you can stand again.

Know that it is I who gives you strength, I and no other. I am the one who makes your way, straightens your path, removes your obstacles. I am the One through whom you have the access to strength and power. I am the One who will save you from all things—at times, even yourself—and all because I love you. You are the apple of My eye. You are My delight.

I will make your way sure and true. But you must seek Me. Walk with Me. And believe that I know best. Believe that when you are in Me, your desires meet with Mine—and they will be fulfilled.

Eternal Partners

And Ruth said, Urge me not to leave you or to turn back from following you;
for where you go I will go, and where you lodge I will lodge.
Your people shall be my people and your God my God.
RUTH 1:16 AMPC

In pain or loss, in sickness and in health I am with you. I will never leave you nor forsake you. Plant this thought firmly in your mind. Know that My power and strength never leave you. Both lie within you, ready to be brought to the fore by your remembrance of Me, your acknowledgment of Me and My way in your life. Do you not see this?

Thus there is no room for despair, no place for fear or discouragement. For I am your all in all. There is nothing that can separate us—but you.

Be as steadfast in your devotion to Me as Ruth to Naomi. Be as determined to go with Me, letting nothing part us. No matter how unsure you are, no matter how limited your sight, depend on Me. Make Me your assurance, your vision maker. Put your hand in Mine. Stick with Me—as I stick with you. And you will reach a place of promise, a land of milk and honey where your dreams—and Mine—come true. Eternal partners in God's plan, from beginning to end.

Under His Wings

"I've heard all about you. . .how you left your father and mother. . .and have come to live among a bunch of total strangers. GOD reward you well for what you've done—and with a generous bonus besides from GOD, to whom you've come seeking protection under his wings."
RUTH 2:11–12 MSG

In the eyes of the world, you have taken many risks in following your path, the true path, to the Lord God. You may have had to turn your back on loved ones to be standing beside Me now. Such risks because of such great faith are rewarded by God. Continue to rely on His protection. His promises are always true and fulfilled.

Now that you are here, with Me, endeavor to be surrounded by His people, those who seek what you seek. Be they friends or strangers, when standing with them, you will find the support and power to carry out My plans for you. You will find the family you need, a family like no other—God's family.

Here, under God's wings, you are in a place of security, protection, defense. You are shielded from all that would harm you. Here there is nothing to fear or stress over. Here you can rest, knowing you are guarded day and night. You have done well, little bird. Rest.

Sit Still

*Then she said, "Sit still, my daughter, until you
know how the matter will turn out."*
RUTH 3:18 NKJV

⸺◦⬦◦⸺

You have listened. You have labored. You have obeyed. You have done all that you could. Now is the time to sit back. Patiently wait. Know that all things are in My hands. Trust that no matter what happens, I alone know best. Be still within until you know how things will turn out.

Walk with Me beside the calm waters. Stop to rest, to sit down on the lush grass. Put all your expectations in My hands. Breathe deep. Relax your body. Allow My peace to fill you from top to bottom. Feel My Spirit calming you. Allow the songs of nature to fill your thoughts. Feel the sunlight on your face, warming you. Stay in this state of peacefulness as you go about your day.

Carry this aura of stillness around with you. Continue to breathe in My love, peace, and light. Know, rest in the assurance that you will soon know how everything will turn out. The matter is now in My hands, exactly where it needs—and is meant—to be.

....
....
....
....
....
....
....
....
....
....

*For the vision is yet for an appointed time and it hastens to the end [fulfillment];
it will not deceive or disappoint. Though it tarry, wait [earnestly] for it,
because it will surely come; it will not be behindhand on its appointed day.*
HABAKKUK 2:3 AMPC

Really Believe

*And Jesus answered them, Truly I say to you, if you have faith (a firm relying trust)
and do not doubt, you will not only do what has been done to the fig tree, but even if
you say to this mountain, Be taken up and cast into the sea, it will be done. And whatever
you ask for in prayer, having faith and [really] believing, you will receive.*
MATTHEW 21:21–22 AMPC

An amazing path, an amazing prospect, lies before you. But to embark upon it, you must believe in Me—truly believe in Me. There must be no doubt. No faltering. No what-ifs, no maybes crowding your mind. Are you there? Do you have this belief? Are you seeing with the eyes of faith what is not yet a reality?

Remember Thomas, the one who doubted that it was truly Me who stood before him in resurrected form? The one who insisted on seeing My hands and My feet before he would take Me at My word? It was to him that I said, "Blessed are they who believe without seeing." Those words spoken thousands of years ago were meant for you.

Really believe and keep on believing. And you will receive and keep on receiving. Amazing things await you on your walk with Me, as you take Me at My Word.

Refuge

My soul takes refuge and finds shelter and confidence in You;
yes, in the shadow of Your wings will I take refuge and be
confident until calamities and destructive storms are passed.
PSALM 57:1 AMPC

Come, fly with Me above the cares of this world. Come up high, above all your troubles, the world's woes, and sit with Me here in this place, where you can breathe and find safety beneath God's wings. Rest, confident that all will be well. Gain the knowledge and peace you need for whatever may come. Know that you will have the strength for all things, because you have spent these precious moments with Me.

Seek Me as your shelter in all areas of life, at all times during the day. Imagine I am an invisible and invincible shield surrounding you. Nothing can touch you, that is the strength of My power and your place in My plan. I am your safe harbor where you can wait out all storms that cross your path. With Me, there are no unchartered waters on your course. Simply trust. Know you are on the right path. Just wait things out until the waters are calmer, until you can weigh anchor and set sail again.

And there shall be a pavilion for shade in the daytime from the heat,
and for a place of refuge and a shelter from storm and from rain.
ISAIAH 4:6 AMPC

Unlimited Vision

*Thus says the Lord Who made [the earth]. . . Call to Me and I will answer you
and show you great and mighty things, fenced in and hidden, which you do not
know (do not distinguish and recognize, have knowledge of and understand).*
JEREMIAH 33:2–3 AMPC

Remove yourself from the whirlwind of worry and call on Me. Seek My face. Delve into My Word. Ask Me what you would wish to know. Expect an answer.

There are so many things you do not—cannot—see. Things that are beyond your knowledge. Things that only I can understand. And this is how it should be, for I am a power so much greater than you. Rest in the comfort of knowing that I—the One who created all things, even you—am so much more powerful and all knowing than you. I put boundaries on the oceans and the sky. I spoke and the darkness abated. I enlightened the world. I see things with a God-perspective. I have unlimited vision. And I have all things under control.

If you are seeking knowledge or insight, come to Me. Pray to Me. Leave your question in My hands. Know that I will provide an answer when the time is right. When you are ready. Until then, I am here to comfort, guide, and direct you in all things. Trust in Me.

The Task at Hand

Be strong, alert, and courageous, O Zerubbabel, says the Lord; be strong, alert, and courageous,
O Joshua. . .and be strong, alert, and courageous, all you people of the land, says the Lord,
and work! For I am with you. . . . According to the promise that I covenanted with you when
you came out of Egypt, so My Spirit stands and abides in the midst of you; fear not.
Haggai 2:4–5 ampc

Times past are just that—past. Do no backward looking. Forget about how wonderful things used to be, how magnificent. Each stage has its heyday. But backward glances keep you from focusing on the task at hand.

Here and now is the time to cast off your weaknesses, inattentiveness, and fears. In their place, cast on strength, awareness, and courage. Remember that I never change. And to this day I am standing in your midst, ready to help you do the best you can with what you have.

All the things I have promised you are yours—if only you would trust Me and work with Me. So pray for all the strength and courage you need to complete the task before you. Then, knowing I have heard your pleas, lift up your hands. Get to work. I will help you every step of the way.

Look for Me

So they went out in the boat, but they caught nothing all night. At dawn Jesus was standing on the beach. . . . He said, "Throw out your net on the right-hand side of the boat, and you'll get some!" So they did, and they couldn't haul in the net because there were so many fish in it.

JOHN 21:3–4, 6 NLT

Know that when your endeavors have brought up nothing, when you have failed at something to which you have put your hand, I will show up. I will be there. I will be standing at the edge of the water, watching, asking how things are going.

When you admit your shortcomings and how things did not go as planned, when you are at your lowest, weakest point in any endeavor, I am there to give you guidance, to tell you where to cast down your net. I will give you specific instructions on what to do next, no matter how hopeless the prospect or how futile My advice seems.

It is then, when you choose to obey My voice, to go against common sense, that you will not only succeed but recognize where your success and strength and profit come from: Me.

So look for Me in all you do. Obey My instructions. Seek to recognize My hand—even where and when you least expect it working. Praise Me for your provision. Commune with Me. And you will find your reward—in heaven and on earth.

Quieted Soul

Lord, my heart is not haughty, nor my eyes lofty; neither do I exercise myself in matters too great or in things too wonderful for me. Surely I have calmed and quieted my soul; like a weaned child with his mother, like a weaned child is my soul within me [ceased from fretting].
PSALM 131:1–2 AMPC

Breathe deep. Allow all the thoughts of what's happening in the world and in your life to drift away. Fill your mind with My promises—to love, protect, defend, bless, and strengthen you. Things I have done since before you were even born.

When change comes, do not mourn for what has passed. Instead, calm yourself. Cease from worrying, from longing for what is no longer. Consider that now your hands and heart have more room to hold what is to come.

Give thought to the hope you have in Me, the expectation of what God has for you. Feed your thoughts and spirit on the confidence you have in Us. Move away from what was; be content with what is, and look forward to what will be, allowing your spirit to soar with a new vision.

O Israel, hope in the Lord from this time forth and forever.
PSALM 131:3 AMPC

God's Gifts

God has given each of you a gift from his great variety of spiritual gifts. Use them well to serve one another. . . . Do it with all the strength and energy that God supplies. Then everything you do will bring glory to God through Jesus Christ.

1 PETER 4:10–11 NLT

───◦◆◦───

When you are at your lowest is often a time for you to rise to the heights. This is done by pouring your life into service for another. In this way, you forget your own sorrows, troubles, anxieties.

I can provide all the strength and energy you desire. And as you use your God-given gift to help another soul, you will find yourself inspired, taken out of yourself, beyond what you could have hoped or desired, beyond what you could have done to rescue yourself.

Remember, I am your Savior. I can lift you up out of the pit of despair, and soon you will be riding upon the heights of heaven with Me. The wind we ride upon is love for others. Empowered by the Spirit, there is nothing that, together, we cannot do.

So in all ways and in all days, serve other souls. Give them the gift of My love. Become an ever-shining beacon of My light. Help someone who cannot help himself, and in doing so, bring glory to Me.

Expect Me. . .

The Lord will command His loving-kindness in the daytime, and in the night His song
shall be with me, a prayer to the God of my life. . . . Hope in God and wait expectantly
for Him, for I shall yet praise Him, Who is the help of my countenance, and my God.
PSALM 42:8, 11 AMPC

Know that each and every moment of the day I am pouring My love out upon you. Feel it surrounding you, enveloping you, sustaining you. And when you go to lie down at night, know that I am still with you, cradling you in My arms, singing you to sleep. I will carry you off to a place of quiet and rest, of light and love, of steadiness and strength, nurturing you, renewing you, speaking into your dreams.

Listen for Me calling you, deep to deep, Spirit to spirit. I am here beside you. Simply speak, whisper, think My name, *Jesus,* and I will make My presence known no matter where you are. Know that I have already prepared the path that you are on. I am walking with you, staying true to My promise to never leave nor forsake you. Feel Me next to you, holding your hand, loving you, leading you, inspiring you, lifting you up out of yourself and ever closer to God. Expect Me, and I am there.